take back your *life*

take back
your *life*

A Caregiver's Guide to Finding
Freedom in the Midst of Overwhelm

LOREN M. GELBERG-GOFF, LCSW

WELL WITHIN PUBLISHING

Dedicated to my amazing children, Cheryl and Elliott, who have taught me the challenges and joys of parenthood and have shown incredible love, devotion, and resilience through our journey together.

To my husband, Lloyd, who never lost his spirit for life: TGIA (Thank God I'm Alive).

To all caregivers who give selflessly of themselves to those they love: You have my admiration, appreciation, and gratitude for all I have learned from you.

Contents

Contents

Introduction

I BEGAN MY CAREER IN social work more than thirty-five years ago, working with terminally and chronically ill individuals and their families. This work took place in hospitals, clinics, hospices, adult day programs, and ultimately in my private practice. I saw what it took for both patients and their families to find the means to be resilient in the face of the many challenges that came with a serious diagnosis, looking at a lifetime of caring for a disabled child, or facing the end of life. I helped family caregivers deal with the enormous responsibilities that they faced every day and learned the importance of self-care: that it really isn't selfishness; *it is self-preservation*. I loved my work, I respected and cared about my clients, and I discovered that this was incredibly important and necessary work, even more than I had realized going into my profession.

Then, out of nowhere, in 1997, my husband became disabled. He experienced constant, excruciating pain and was unable to work. This began our family's immersion in a world I had been professionally engaged in for almost twenty years. We had two young children (ages eleven and four) to love and care for as well as a home and my career to manage. I now had to walk the talk I had been practicing. The world looked different from the inside, as every caregiver knows. I thought I would be immune from the pitfalls so many caregivers experience, because I understood this world. I was in for a very intense awakening.

I learned to be very organized; operated on autopilot; compensated for my husband's significant limitations; took on ever-growing responsibilities, demands, and obligations; and resisted asking for the help that would have made my life easier and more balanced. I learned what it felt like to be a martyr, and, as you know all too well, there is no joy in martyrdom. While my practice had been thriving for many years, in 2013 I knew I had to do one more thing. I created the powerful and life-changing program for caregivers, Take Back Your Life: The Art of Self-Care. This program guides caregivers to live free of chronic, daily anxiety, and overwhelm without having to constantly feel guilty, angry, and resentful.

In 2013, my parents' health and physical abilities took a downturn. They needed to downsize, and we helped them move into an independent-living building where they managed fairly well, with help, for over a year. As their needs increased, their help at home increased as well, and my younger sister was able to increase her involvement. She went with them to doctors' appointments, managed their medications, visited them daily, handled their finances, and was completely devoted to them every step of the way.

My older sister and I each had our roles as well, as our parents' needs continued to grow unabated. We learned and respected each other's strengths and learned to communicate with each other in new ways to best meet our parents' needs and our desired outcomes. My parents struggled at times with their declining abilities and the fact that they needed so much help. They were also able to express gratitude for the love and care they received.

Everyone is not so lucky to experience the good, since so many aging, frail parents resist help, express a great deal of anger at their limitations, and take their anger out on those they love the most.

My parents passed away within six months of each other in 2015. The work and relationship between my sisters and me continues to evolve, as is true for all families who are creating new, healthy, adult relationships. This is an offshoot of caregiving and learning to take as good care of yourself as you do of the others in your life. Although this has been my career for decades, it's always different when you're doing it for yourself. Reaching out to get the necessary and deserved support is imperative.

My husband's disability has been a constant source of learning, growing, and evolving for him, our children (who are now adults), and for me. We were blessed to have found an amazing physical therapist who introduced us to cold laser therapy, through which, miraculously, after intensive and extensive treatments, my husband is now pain-free. This has given him back a huge portion of his life, which he had lost over the past twenty years.

His pain began receding two years ago, and he is now off all pain medications, which is an enormous blessing on many levels. He is working on reintegrating into the daily rhythm of our lives, which has changed over the past two decades, and that is a process which also requires many of the coping strategies, skills, and tools that we work on in the Take Back Your Life group program. He is able to work part-time now, and he is so very grateful to be able to provide meaningful and worthwhile services that make a difference.

There is no right or wrong way to read this book. It is meant to provide guidance, support, and encouragement on your journey as a caregiver. You may choose to read this book and do the workbook pages straight through from beginning to end, or you may find yourself struggling with a particular issue and open up to that chapter for the guidance you need. You might even choose to pull out the Step-by-Step Guide and work through the issue you are facing in order to get started right away, on making changes in how you take care of yourself with the love, respect, and compassion that you so richly need and deserve.

Throughout the book you will read the phrase "and we breathe." It is a phrase I use as a reminder to catch my breath and pause to prevent reacting and allow space for responding to situations that cause stress, upset tension, and aggravation. I explain its use throughout the book, and I hope you will find it both useful and beneficial on your journey to take as loving care of yourself as you do of others in your life.

Life is a constant, ever-evolving journey full of learning opportunities, challenges, and wonderful celebrations, if we allow them. I am grateful for all the curves in the road that I have experienced and that I am able to bring my professional expertise, my personal experiences, and my years of learning to the caregivers who are the unsung heroes every day. I am grateful for all I have learned from every caregiver I have worked with over the past thirty-five years. Thank you.

And we breathe...

Chapter 1
My Desired Outcome

Your own self-realization is the greatest
service you can render the world.

—Ramona Maharshi, modern Indian guru

Do you know the exact moment you became a caregiver? Was it a sudden crisis or did your role evolve over time? Have you always been the one everyone counted on to help out, or was this role thrust upon you? Whatever the occurrence, what may have started as an acute, short-term condition has now evolved into a long-term, chronic situation and lifestyle. For me, it was three months after my husband's surgery, when we realized that he would not recover normal functioning, would not be able to return to work, and that he now had severe, debilitating nerve pain that interfered with all his activities and severely limited his ability to participate in life.

Most of us can handle anything for a limited period of time: running extra errands, spending time at the hospital, taking on extra responsibilities, making phone calls and appointments. Over time, though, having to reconfigure your days and even your nights can become an exhausting and overwhelming existence. Life is now filled with a never-ending stream of demands, needs, and obligations to someone else, or maybe even more than one person, and it is nearly impossible to think about what else you might want or do.

You're caught in the loop of caregiving and have lost sight of your own needs, feelings, and desires. You've put them on hold until... who knows? Well, we're going to change that overwhelming cycle, and help you find your way out of fatigue and burnout to create fulfillment and empowerment. And, yes, it is possible to take your life back. It begins with one question: *What is my desired outcome?*

Your desired outcome must fulfill two major requirements:

1. It must be something you want, not something you *don't* want and
2. It must be something over which you yourself have control.

What is your desired outcome? is my favorite question, and as you go through this book it may become both your favorite and your most demanding question, one that always requires an answer.

Desired outcomes can be both long-term and short-term goals. They all require small, individual steps that you have to choose to take in order to make them realities. Every situation brings both challenges and opportunities if you are willing to take time to explore and examine what you want, need, and feel. Focusing on a *desired outcome* helps you create a laser-focus on steps you can take to achieve it.

It's important to become clear about what you want in order to move forward in your life with direction and purpose. Otherwise, you may end up floating or struggling through each day feeling unfulfilled, empty, numb, or even depressed—not a very pretty picture.

This habit of blinding ourselves to what we need to feel happy, *right now*, is something of an epidemic in our modern society. How many times have you thought, *Someday, things will be better,* or, *Someday, I'll be able to do what I want,* or, *Someday I'll be able to relax and enjoy life*? How long have you been telling yourself those things, without ever reaching *someday*?

All too often, we are asked what we want, and the answer is "I don't know," or, "It doesn't matter," or maybe even, "I don't know what I want, but I know I don't want _____" (fill in the blank with one of an array of predictable sources of caregiver stress and frustration).

The reason we so readily flip the question to what it is we *don't* want is that most of us have not been taught that it's okay to *want* something. Many of us are taught that it's not *polite* to ask for something and that we should settle for whatever is offered and be grateful for it.

Many women have been taught to defer to their friend, boyfriend, or husband, especially after growing up dutifully deferring to their parents. Often, at best we are only vaguely aware that something is missing. We know there's significant stress or struggle in our lives, but we're not too clear on what we want that could help alleviate the problem, beyond the temporary Band-Aid of one less errand or doctor appointment… or maybe a nap. The story we tell ourselves is that this is all normal or that this is life, and who are we to expect something more?

As you read this book and do the workbook pages, you'll learn to come up with more long-term solutions that are directly based upon your desired outcomes. A desired outcome gives you clarity and direction; even if you're not quite sure how to get where you want to go, a desired outcome gives you something to focus on. This is especially helpful when you're feeling overwhelmed by stress, guilt, and fatigue.

Dr. Martin Luther King, Jr. once said, "Faith is taking the first step even when you can't see the whole staircase." I can confidently predict that once you get clarity on your desired outcome, even if you have no idea how to get there, you will find that first step.

This book is going to open your eyes to new possibilities and new options. It is imperative that you learn to become aware of what it is you want. If you don't acknowledge what you want or need, unless you have someone in your life who is a mind reader, chances are you'll walk around feeling deprived, frustrated, upset, resentful, angry, or even all of these at once.

Let's move forward and change this storyline.

Is This You?

AS A CAREGIVER, YOU HAVE been committed to providing support, compassion, help, and care for someone in your life. If you've been a caregiver for a long time, then some truly significant and powerful habits and beliefs have already set in. Most caregivers, whether they came into this role by choice or by default, are compassionate, nurturing, and selfless individuals. If you are like them, you'd much rather do things for others than have others do anything for you.

You rarely, if ever, actively think about what you want, or need, though it may be a nagging thought or feeling in the recesses of your mind. And when it does pop up as more than a vague awareness, you ignore it, deflect it, silently implode, or—for the moment—loudly explode, and then the cycle resumes. While not very pleasing or inspiring, this has been a pattern in your life. You put one foot in front of the other and just keep on going.

For most caregivers I have worked with, their number one desired outcome, after ensuring their loved one is safe and well cared for, is simply *to get a break*. Yet somehow, getting a break always seems so elusive. They tell me something inevitably pops up to interfere with satisfying even this modest goal.

More distressing, too often over time they start to feel permanently defeated. When there is something that they really want, or when they know they *need* something that seems vital to their health and well-being, even then they are stuck in an old belief and habit that reinforces, *Later, Never mind, It'll never happen,* or, *I'll get a break when* _____, or even the sarcastic, *Who am I kidding?* How many of these expressions of defeat and resignation sound like you?

Here's the reality of a desired outcome:

1. It has to be something you really want, and
2. In order to hope to achieve it, you first have to be aware of it.

Making any kind of change in your life requires conscious and specific acknowledgment of what you are feeling, dealing with, and experiencing. There is no room for minimizing, ignoring, or denying that stressful, overwhelming, and frustrating situations exist. It's time to use these moments as learning opportunities to bring in new awareness, new possibilities, and new outcomes.

Lucy's Story

WHEN I FIRST MET LUCY, she had been responsible for her elderly mother's care for a number of years. Initially, her mother's needs were minimal: primarily emotional demands, complaints about minor inconveniences, and an occasional doctor's visit. Lucy was accustomed to her mother's depressed and demanding nature, so she didn't consider how much of her emotional energy was drained during their interactions.

The result—feeling put out, somewhat annoyed, and frustrated—was a normal state of mind for Lucy. It wasn't until her husband pointed out that they hadn't had a free night or weekend in what felt like *forever* that she suddenly realized the magnitude of the intrusion into the other important areas of her life. Whenever Lucy came to see me she would sit rigidly on the couch, reflecting her intense need for the control that she was clearly not really feeling.

"I think my husband is being overly dramatic and demanding," Lucy told me during a session. Her response didn't surprise me. After all, their life seemed normal to her. Running on a regular basis to handle her mother's latest complaint, demand, or need was par for the course. Lucy hadn't thought about how she was feeling; she was used to a high, ongoing level of stress and tension, especially when it came to dealing with her mother. She hadn't thought about the impact her constant devotion and involvement with her mother had on her marriage and herself.

When I first asked Lucy what her desired outcome was, she said, "I want my husband to be more understanding. It's not like my mother will live forever, and she's all alone—there really isn't anybody else to help out."

I explained that a desired outcome had to be something over which she, herself, had control and her husband being more understanding didn't fit that criterion. Deep breath... So, what was it Lucy wanted? It had been such a long time since she had thought of her own wants and needs, it took her a long time to answer that question. She sat quietly, seemingly holding her breath, and her dismay became evident as tears flooded her eyes.

"My mother really is taking up all of my free time. I can't believe I couldn't see that, and that I didn't notice my husband felt deprived and annoyed," Lucy said finally. At last she acknowledged to herself that there was a real problem. "My desired outcome is," she continued, "I want some time to myself, when I don't have to take care of anything for my mother."

Now that Lucy was aware of the stress and tension that her husband felt, she became aware of her own feelings regarding the time and care that her mother demanded of her. It's not that Lucy wasn't feeling this before, it's that she was so used to living with the ongoing stress and tension that she hadn't allowed it to come into her conscious awareness. She was so worried about everything that her mother needed that she hadn't taken time to think about what *she* might want or need, or that *her* habits *actually mattered* to someone else, especially her husband.

It can't be stressed enough how very common this issue is for caregivers, and that it is something you really can change going forward.

Oftentimes, until you stop and check in with yourself and how you're feeling, autopilot takes over. Asking yourself, *What is my desired outcome?* helps to create conscious awareness. This is critical in the change process in order to break old habits and beliefs. Do you want to? Do you feel ready to embrace the truth that your needs, feelings, and wants really do matter?

Even if, at the moment, you do not know what you specifically want, focus on allowing yourself to feel relaxed, peaceful, empowered, and maybe even deserving of some free time in your life. As you go through this book, you will learn that you have choices and do not have to simply accept what is and what has been.

Being open to and embracing change is not easy, but every challenge you face in life that you don't automatically dismiss or shy away from helps you to learn, grow, and evolve. Take a deep breath and give yourself permission to face and overcome the habits and patterns that have become your life as a caregiver. It's normal to feel fear when embarking on something new in your life, but fear does not mean *Don't do it*. It means, *Proceed with awareness and with conscious purpose.* You can now consciously choose how you want to care for yourself while you are still caring for others.

Lucy was able to awaken to new possibilities in her life, including spending more time with her husband, exploring new options for handling her mother's needs and demands, and recognizing that she needed to take better care of herself. Lucy actually smiles now; she can sit relaxing on the couch as she shares stories about time with friends and weekends with her husband, and she breathes more easily as she describes not running in response to every demand her mother makes.

Lucy says quite frequently, with awe in her voice, "I cannot believe the change in me and in my life." She says that she still shakes her head in gratitude that she can enjoy some of her visits with her mother as well. As Lucy put it one day, "What a concept!"

Asking yourself, *What is my desired outcome?* and taking the steps that follow in this book is where self-care begins: within yourself, in your heart, in your mind and in your soul.

My desired outcome for this book is to provide you with strategies, tools, support, and encouragement that you can use, so that you really can take as good care of yourself as you do of others in your life. You deserve this, and now is the time. Remember, it's only too late if you don't start now.

And we breathe...

Chapter 1 Worksheet

What is Your Desired Outcome?

1. List my desired outcome(s). "I can take as good care of myself as I do of those I love and care for." My desired outcome has to be what I want and has to be something over which I have control.

   _____

   _____

   _____

   _____

2. What are the circumstances or situations that interfere with my desired outcomes and how are they contributing to the ongoing cycle of deprivation, overwhelm, and guilt?

   _____

   _____

   _____

   _____

3. What changes am I willing to implement in my life that will reduce or eliminate my feeling overwhelmed, stressed, and burnt out?

   _____

   _____

   _____

   _____

4. What specific beliefs do I hold that contribute to the cycle of deprivation, overwhelm, and guilt?

_____

_____

_____

_____

5. What new beliefs am I willing to embrace and practice to end the cycle of deprivation, overwhelm, and guilt?

_____

_____

_____

_____

You can download the Caregiver's Step-by-Step Guide or see Appendix 1 to help you on your journey of learning to take as good care of yourself as you do of others in your life. You can find the guide at www.lorenGelbergGoff.com/sbsg-tbyl.

More Tools for Change:
Emotional Freedom Contract with Myself
*My reminder to take as good care of myself
as I do of others… I matter*

I, _____, RECOGNIZE MYSELF AS an adult with options and choices and I commit to the process of actively taking care of myself with respect, consideration, and compassion. In order to achieve this desired outcome, I make the following promises to myself:

1. I promise to *Stop! Breathe!* and *Focus!* so that I am better able to choose to ask for and expect the respect I deserve, and better able to see how I allow others to treat me.

2. I promise to respond to situations with clarity, respect, and love for myself, knowing that each time I am able to do this, I am one step closer to living my truth, that *who I am is enough.*

3. I promise myself that when I slip into old habits along the way, I will *not* beat myself up. I will learn and grow from the experience.

4. As I work through this process of taking my life back (and beyond), I promise to treat myself with the love, respect, and compassion that I deserve.

5. I promise to recognize the importance of caring for myself and focusing on my desired outcomes while respecting others' feelings and opinions.

6. I promise I will acknowledge and appreciate myself for each positive step along this journey, no matter how small each step may seem.

7. I remind myself each and every day that I can and do cope with the circumstances in my life with empowerment, *not* martyrdom.

In moments of stress, tension, and uncertainty, especially when interacting with others, take a deep breath and say the following:

I treat myself with the love, respect, and acceptance I deserve and I teach others that I expect the same from them.

Chapter 2
From Deprivation to Self-Care:
No Longer Taking on What Isn't Mine

*I recognize those tasks that do not have to
belong to me and respectfully find ways to
let go and delegate.*

A DAY OR SO AFTER Hurricane Floyd tore through the East
Coast, my daughter, Cheryl, asked me if I would please drive her
to a friend's house that was about two-and-a-half miles away. I
was reluctant to do it, as there was a great deal of flooding and
tree damage. Cheryl begged and pleaded, and, against my better
judgment, I relented and agreed to drive her there. You see, because
I always wanted to compensate for what my husband was unable
to do or participate in, I found it difficult to refuse what seemed
like simple requests from either of my children. (Sound familiar?)
By this time in the caregiving process with her father's disability,
I was just doing what was asked of me. It often seemed easier to
say yes to maintain equilibrium in our home.

Once we were on the road, I had to navigate around the downed
trees and power lines and avoid the floods on the roads. I was very
wary of the heavy winds, which shook the car.

My voice filled with sheer exasperation and frustration, I said,
"Honey, this is totally insane! I don't know why we're doing this."

In an instant, Cheryl's response jolted me back to a saner mindset and awareness. "You know, Mom, you could have said no."

I took a slow, deep breath. A change in my perspective and attitude had to be made—and it only took driving through the dangerous aftermath of a hurricane to come to that conclusion!

It's All On Me

FOR ANYONE WHO HAS EVER flown on an airplane, you know that when the flight attendants are reviewing safety and emergency procedures, they will tell you that, should oxygen be required during the flight, oxygen masks will drop down, and, if you are traveling with a dependent, you are to place your own oxygen mask over your face first. This is a request that initially seems very counterintuitive. However, the reality is, if *you* are not breathing, then you will be unable to assist the very person or people you love. Deprivation grows from the feeling that everyone else has to have oxygen before you do. You really can reduce feelings of deprivation when you actually stop and take in your oxygen.

Whatever you've been doing in your caregiving duties, responsibilities or obligations may have started in small, insidious ways. Perhaps it started out as a temporary, stop-gap measure and became long-term. Maybe you took on responsibilities because you didn't think about asking anyone else to help. You might not have known that you could ask for help or that there was even anyone to ask.

Maybe your role as a caregiver gave you a sense of importance and control in your family. To be valued, appreciated, and in control is a very heady feeling and one that becomes increasingly addictive—until it loses its sheen. When it does, whatever the reasons may be for taking on as much as you have, something has shifted for you so that you are not feeling the same degree of reward in your role as caregiver. Most people don't change their behaviors unless a catalyst, be it internal or external, forces us to change. It is then we usually experience fear, anger, trepidation, anxiety, uncertainty, and—let's not forget—guilt.

How did you become a caregiver? Have you always taken better care of others than of yourself? Are you the one who cringes at the thought of placing the oxygen mask over your face first? When did that start? These are very important questions because they will help you to look at what patterns have developed for you as well as for the people in your life. You've created patterns of behavior that others have come to expect and rely on, and they may react with anger, surprise, disappointment, maybe even guilt trips when you express even the possibility of changing your behavior.

If you've become fearful of others' reactions to you making changes, then you will not make the changes necessary to take back your power and reclaim your life. This is *not* about not caring for anyone else anymore; it's about making sure *you* appear on your list of priorities. When you look at your list of responsibilities for any given day, where do your needs show up? Do they show up at all? Do you consider taking care of yourself a responsibility you have?

All this is hard enough when the person you are caring for lives under the same roof, but what happens when you have to include running back and forth to the other person's home in your day? Now you have to tack on even more booked time, adding exponentially to your stress and responsibilities.

Have any of the following thoughts run through your head?

- There's no one else who can do this.
- It's all on me.
- It would be too burdensome to have to teach someone else to handle all this.
- It's just quicker if I do it myself.
- He/she won't let anyone else do this.

And the list goes on and on. These are all beliefs that keep you stuck on the path of being and feeling overworked, overburdened, and overstressed. Are you ready to explore a few new thoughts, beliefs, and behaviors?

Ask yourself, *When did I become the keeper of everyone's life?* Is this a relatively new phenomenon or a role you've played in your life? Allow yourself to sit with this question. Don't judge it or analyze it, just become aware of how entrenched your belief is that you are responsible for everyone and everything and that somehow you haven't done your job properly if something goes wrong. Remember, I am not saying you are responsible for nothing; I am saying that you are *not* responsible for *everything*.

Our beliefs determine our words and actions. Often we are not consciously aware of our beliefs; we simply operate on autopilot. This is all about putting one foot in front of the other just to get through the day. One woman used to refer to her caregiving responsibilities as "soldiering on." As long as she didn't stop to think about how busy and overwhelmed she felt, maybe it wouldn't really count. Denial is a powerful defense mechanism, and its purpose is to keep us from facing realities that feel so scary, overwhelming, and frustrating that we deny, ignore, and hide from them and "soldier on" through the next day, and the next.

Are you feeling the familiar sensation of being burdened, stressed, and tense? How often do people in your life do something that causes a problem and you immediately sink into the feeling that there should have been some way for you to prevent this problem, that you should have seen it coming, that there should be something that you could do to undo the problem that has now been created? Whenever you feel this way: *Stop! Breathe! Focus!*

The Never-ending List

AS A CAREGIVER, THERE ARE many things for which you are responsible. You may be the keeper of schedules, medications, appointments, chauffeuring, household maintenance, shopping, cooking, cleaning, and emergencies. Chances are you are responsible for all this and more. Somehow, as a caregiver, the list of responsibilities seems never-ending and ever-growing. Since you are reading this book, some part of you wants to change this.

You take on a lot, and it may seem that, without your responsible qualities, capabilities, helpfulness, compassion, and managerial skills, all would be lost. Do you worry about who would pay the bills, make and keep doctor or therapy appointments, make sure there's food in the refrigerator, and ensure that your own family schedules are kept? This list of all that we fear would be lost seems to go on in a never-ending stream.

By definition, caregivers give and do an enormous amount. Whether you are a family member providing care or a professional whose job it is to provide care, recognizing what is legitimately your responsibility and what is not is critical to your overall health and well-being. I'll talk more about boundaries in the next chapter, but for now, become consciously aware of everything that you handle and everything that people ask of you or just expect you to handle. It will be helpful if you write down everything that you take care of and everything for which you feel responsible. Remember the little things, like getting to the grocery store, going to the dry cleaners, doing laundry, fixing dinner (as if there's time), picking up prescriptions, attending back-to-school nights and sports events for children or grandchildren, getting your hair done (yes, that's important, too), taking the trash out… I feel your exhaustion.

The purpose of making this list is not to give you something else to do; goodness knows your to-do list is long enough. It is intended to give you clarity as to what it is you take on in a given day. Before any changes can be made, you need to have awareness so that you can decide, from a conscious space, what you would like to give up, change, or keep. There may be parts of the caregiving role that you enjoy, feel good about, or want to do. I know I felt good that I was knowledgeable about home-care resources for my parents. Making a difference in my husband's overall feelings of well-being in spite of his chronic debilitating pain felt empowering, and it felt good that I could do some reflexology, which helped my parents and my husband feel relaxed and even helped them sleep better.

My goal here is to help you focus on how to bring more of what you feel good about into your life and let go of what depletes you. Caregiving, as I stated earlier, is all about giving, and the goal here is to help you bring some balance into your life so that you can also receive.

All relationships are about balance. Remember seesaws from your childhood? Remember how you would work to create that perfect balance and what would happen when one person suddenly shifted her weight, sending the other person on the seesaw flying up into the air or plunging to the ground? Our relationships are similar to that scenario. Everything we do is to create a balance; the purpose here is to be able to balance giving with receiving.

If you find that, as a caregiver, you take on more and more and others in your life do less and less, this is also a way of maintaining balance and equilibrium. Since you have taken on so much, others are able to do less and less. This is how the balancing act works. If you are the one keeping track of all appointments, then no one else has to. If you are the one remembering the timing for medications, then no one else has to. The more you do the same thing over and over, the more tedious, exhausting, burdensome, and annoying it may become, though it may have started out seeming like "no big deal". Consequently, as you have taken on more and more, and others have had to do less and less, a balance of imbalance is established.

Just as you might remember the tension you would feel while sitting upon the seesaw, wondering when the other person would upset the delicate balance that had been established, so, too, it is in life. If you are doing something that you know you really don't want to do, rest assured that as long as you continue to provide that service, no else has to. Do you see the other people in your life as unavailable, too busy, distant, or unhelpful? Do you get the message that they "can't" help out? Do you then feel stuck with the responsibilities that have fallen to you?

As long as you believe that there is no one else to help, that will be your ongoing reality.

Are You in a State of Deprivation?

THE QUESTION, *WHAT IS YOUR desired outcome?*—as I discussed in Chapter 1 and which you will see frequently throughout this book—will become both your favorite and most aggravating question.

It is the question that gets you to focus clearly on what it is you want; it is the question that urges you out of denial and powerlessness. Many people resist this step because it brings into sharp focus what they are feeling and what they need and want, and guides them toward steps they can take to achieve their desired outcomes. In other words, it helps move them out of feeling stuck, powerless, and deprived.

Deprivation is a feeling of absence, loss, or the withholding of something needed.

As caregivers, when you are constantly giving to those you love and care for, the feeling of deprivation or a void often takes a long time to emerge. This means that by the time you actually acknowledge that you feel deprived, it's no longer a new feeling, but one you have gotten used to and maybe are numb to.

The first step in being able to deal with deprivation is your willingness to admit it and identify what you miss, what you need, and what you'd like. Many caregivers are afraid to admit to feeling deprived because it brings up feelings of inadequacy, imperfection, or weakness and vulnerability. As a caregiver, you have risen to the challenge of providing for others. Somehow, though you would allow someone else to do less, take a break, and feel vulnerable, you do not give yourself the same consideration, compassion, and care. This attitude and habit stop here! Think about the following statement by David Stafford, from his book *Codependency: How to Break Free and Live Your Own Life*: "Whenever you feel compelled to put others first at the expense of yourself, you are denying your own reality, your own identity." Makes sense, right?

We cannot control everything. What we can control, however, is our response to situations that are out of our control. We can take ownership of our thoughts and feelings without explaining, defending, or justifying them to anyone. Here you are, stretched to your limit, and a relative recommends that you try this new therapy for your mom. They describe it as easy, but you know it's a major time commitment for you, and the one thing you do not have is more time. You would love to explore something that might be beneficial for your mother, but you are already totally overwhelmed and overbooked. This situation triggers feelings of frustration, annoyance, and guilt. And we breathe...

We cannot control what others may ask, recommend, or suggest, but we can most definitely control our responses. People can ask for whatever they want, and we cannot control that, but we can control how we respond to their requests. Without explaining, defending, or justifying your answer, you might say, "Thank you, I appreciate your concern and your idea. Maybe it's something *you* can do with and for Mom." (I'll discuss more about boundaries and limits going forward.) The important point here is to breathe and not get caught in the habit of taking on more and more because you feel obligated, guilty, or defensive, thinking that if you say no you're falling down on the job.

You cannot move forward if you do not allow yourself to be conscious and aware of your feelings, needs, and thoughts and how they make an impact on your choices and decisions.

Carl Jung, the American psychologist who originated the nondirective, or client-centered, approach to psychotherapy, said: "Until we make the unconscious conscious, it will direct our lives and we will call it fate." It's time you step forward out of the fog, frustration, and feelings of being overwhelmed in your daily life. You can own up to what it is you need, want, and deserve. After all, if you are not breathing, not only will you fall apart, but those you care for will fall apart as well.

In order to move out of a state of deprivation and the belief that self-care is selfishness, we have to adopt a new perspective: *Self-care is* not *selfishness; it is self-preservation.* This is the next step on your journey to take back your life.

The following are signs that you have fallen into a state of deprivation. How many of them aptly describe you?

1. **You don't express your needs.** Refusing to express your needs virtually guarantees deprivation. Millions of people allow others to ignore, take advantage, and take them for granted because they will not speak up or believe that they should not speak up.
2. **You are overly focused on the needs of others.** Focusing solely on the needs of others at your own expense is actually a disservice to yourself and others. It typically leads to resentment and emotional martyrdom.
3. **You feel guilty when you do something for yourself.** Feeling guilty or selfish when you meet your own needs is a sign that you don't believe you deserve to have them met.

4. **You can't take compliments.** Not accepting compliments graciously (inside and out) is a way to deflect them, depriving yourself of the need and desire to be appreciated.

5. **You are afraid to ask for what you want or need.** If you don't ask, the answer is always no. A sure way to *not* to get your needs met is to assume that you're not allowed or that someone else's needs are more important than your own. (I am not referring to emergency situations.) When you are committed to putting everyone else's needs and feelings above yours, you are reinforcing your own sense of deprivation.

6. **You expect disappointment.** When you do not expect a successful outcome, you keep fulfillment at a distance. Going into situations anticipating disappointment becomes a self-fulfilling prophecy.

7. **You don't know what you want or have lost any purpose other than caring for someone.** This is so common. People usually don't think of it this way, but not knowing what you want or even giving yourself permission to think about what else you might want is a way to avoid self-care and self-compassion, which inevitably leads to self-deprivation.

8. **You shy away from intimacy.** When you avoid close relationships or shy away from deeper connections with people, you miss out on this fundamental contribution to happiness and fulfillment. Does being busy and occupied with your responsibilities as a caregiver keep your other relationships at a distance, even those with your spouse, children, and friends?

9. **You cannot enjoy the moment.** Letting go and having fun in the here and now is an important way to experience fulfillment and reduce stress. It is a huge need! Focusing always on your responsibilities and commitments and remaining preoccupied robs you of the opportunity to enjoy yourself and your life in the present moment.

All too often, we stay stuck in the stress and overwhelming responsibility of caregiving because no one has given us permission to do anything differently. We don't know that we're allowed to take time, ask for help, or change the rules that we've been following. In this way, we become numb to our sadness, our hurt, our anger, and our resentment. We operate on autopilot and put one foot in front of another to make it through each day, only to collapse at night spent and exhausted, with nothing left to give.

In what ways have you become "mechanized" or robotic, ignoring your own feelings in order to care for others? How often do you put your feelings aside for a job, for peace within the family, or to maintain the status quo? Through your journaling in the workbook pages, let's put some heart and soul back into your day, back into your nights, back into your life.

To step out of deprivation and reconnect to your heart center, your spirit, and make a loving connection to those you love, it's imperative that you understand the importance of self-compassion.

Self-Compassion Consists of a Few Basic Qualities:

1. **Courage to be imperfect.** It's important to allow for the reality that you do not have to be perfect. You do not have

to do everything, have every answer, and prevent every problem. Allowing yourself to be imperfect takes courage to let go of others' judgments as well as the judgments you carry within you. Allow yourself the truth and freedom of being perfectly imperfect.

2. **Connection**. You need the willingness and desire to be genuinely connected to others to prevent feelings of isolation and martyrdom.

3. **Vulnerability**. Being vulnerable is what makes you beautiful. It is acceptable to not have all the answers. It's okay to ask for and receive help. You cannot and do not have to do it all. Vulnerability means you are willing to do something and participate even when there are no guarantees for success. It means you can have and express your feelings of uncertainty, upset, frustration, and even anger.

Sometimes asking for help is the most
meaningful example of self-reliance.

—Anonymous

WE OFTEN AVOID OUR OWN vulnerability by numbing out. We blame others or circumstances for problems and obstacles as a way to discharge our pain and discomfort. You learned somewhere along the line that you had to do it all, manage it all, and make sure everything went along without a hitch. I can tell you here and now that that is an impossible task. (This is something you probably already know, but many resist admitting.)

It's time to reconnect to your heart, to what you want, need, love, and deserve. You already have the wisdom and courage within you. It's accessing them in your daily life that makes a difference to you as you move forward. Making changes in your life means other people, who are used to you doing what they want, when they want it, and how they want it, are likely to be confused, upset, frustrated, or angry about these changes. We'll deal more extensively with the issue of boundaries in the next chapter.

In life we have results or excuses. So, I'll ask you here: What is your desired outcome?

Are you ready to embrace the idea of placing the oxygen mask on your face?

Are you feeling inspired that you can, in fact, make yourself a priority?

Time to look at the workbook pages and honestly answer the questions so that you can move forward to take back your life.

And we breathe...

Chapter 2 Worksheet

From Deprivation to Self-Care:
No Longer Taking on What Isn't Mine

1. Where do I feel deprived in my life today that is contributing to my feelings of guilt and overwhelm? (Be specific and list what you feel is missing for you.)

   _____

   _____

   _____

   _____

2. What do I need or want in my life to counteract my feelings of deprivation? (Again, be specific.)

   _____

   _____

   _____

3. What do I need to eliminate in my life to counteract my feelings of deprivation? (No judgments; just awareness. No "should;" just honesty, for yourself.)

   _____

   _____

   _____

4. What is keeping me stuck in patterns of deprivation, overwhelm, and guilt? (No judgments; just awareness.)

_____

_____

_____

_____

More Tools for Change: Affirmation for Self-Care

I lovingly ask for and accept the help, support, and guidance from others in my life because I know that who I am is enough and, as I relinquish my need to control everything, I make room for greater ease in my life. This is a gift of self-care that I lovingly and willingly give myself.

1. Start and end the affirmation with a slow, deep breath.
2. Don't rush it; say it slowly.
3. Say the affirmation upon waking in the morning, at least three times during the day, and before bed.
4. Jot down your thoughts and feelings each time you say this and notice if they change, and how they change, as the week goes on.
5. Make no judgments, only cultivate awareness.
6. Allow yourself to actually look at what you will let go of, what you would like help with, and what you would want support or guidance with.

7. Use the Caregiver's Step-by-Step Guide to gain clarity and focus. (Download at www.lorenGelbergGoff.com/sbsg-tbyl or see Appendix 1.)
8. As always, remember to *breathe!*

Chapter 3
Boundaries: Setting and Maintaining Healthy Limits

When we fail to set boundaries and hold people
accountable, we feel used and mistreated.
This is why we sometimes attack who they are,
which is far more hurtful than addressing
a behavior or a choice.

—Brené Brown, The Gifts of Imperfection: Let
Go of Who You Think You're Supposed to Be
and Embrace Who You Are

IN THE PROCESS OF ENDING the cycle of self-deprivation and being able to let go of those responsibilities and obligations that are not yours, the topic of boundaries is an imperative issue to explore.

Let's start with the definition of a boundary as laid out by guideposttopsychology.com: *A boundary is anything that marks a limit. Psychological limits define personal dignity.* Healthy boundaries are derived from a place of love, not fear or anger.

The core purpose of a boundary is to defend one's own dignity, and refusing to set a boundary is really based upon disregard for yourself as well as others. Most caregivers do not set healthy boundaries out of fear of upsetting or annoying someone else. You don't set boundaries because you don't want to upset the equilibrium of any given situation. You believe that it's easier to go along than it is to assert yourself, your needs, or your feelings. This is truly problematic if you are going to live the truth that *you matter*.

Setting boundaries means you are taking care of and respecting yourself. Recognizing that boundaries are necessary involves being willing to look at options for any given situation. When it feels too painful to say *no*, to make a change in the status quo, it's imperative to look at what happens to you. Symptoms of not setting boundaries occur in many forms. A few examples are:

- You are used to having a stomachache.
- You feel exhausted and powerless.
- You often think: *What difference does it make?*
- You justify other people's behaviors to avoid conflict.
- You take responsibility for others' behaviors.
- You feel guilty when you say "no", or you say "yes" when you want to say "no."
- You feel uncomfortable in a situation, but ignore or dismiss your feelings.
- You find yourself saying, "It doesn't matter," or, "Who cares," rather than stating your feelings or thoughts.
- You doubt your own opinions or decisions or both.
- You feel resentment toward the people you care for and about.
- You do things to please others that go against your core values and beliefs.
- You are in a constant state of insecurity and uncertainty.

These are just a few signs that something is wrong and a change needs to occur. A boundary needs to be set. *This takes courage.* I know and understand how hard it is to set boundaries when you're used to taking better care of others than you do of yourself. I could feel my own insides twist with the memories of "just letting things slide" when I read the following quote from Henry Cloud and John Townsend's book, *Boundaries*: "When we begin to set boundaries with people we love, a really hard thing happens: They feel hurt. They may feel a hole where you used to plug up their aloneness, their disorganization, or their financial irresponsibility. Whatever it is, they will feel a loss. If you love them, this will be difficult for you to watch. But, when you are dealing with someone who is hurting, remember that your boundaries are both necessary for you and helpful for them. If you have been enabling them to be irresponsible, your limit-setting may nudge them toward responsibility."

If you're not willing to set new boundaries, old patterns will continue and no change will happen. You are the one who has to initiate change because in truth, as Rachel Wolchin, Los Angeles-based writer and blogger observes, "Givers need to set limits because takers rarely do." As a caregiver, you are used to giving, providing, caring, and managing with little or no thought for your own needs and feelings (as discussed in Chapter 2). When you give without care or concern for yourself, you are at risk for significant and severe consequences. There are health consequences when you don't set boundaries and don't make your needs a priority in your life. Stress increases along with the consequences: heart disease, high blood pressure, sleep problems, depression, lowered self-esteem, fatigue, and burnout. If you are not taking care of you, who will?

This is the reality: *You teach others how you are willing to be treated.* When you accept how anyone else behaves without comment or consequence, you are giving them the tacit message that their behavior is acceptable. Even if you complain to your friends or other family members about your mother's (or anyone else's) behavior and how infuriating it is, as long as you continue to tolerate her behavior or attitude, it will continue. Now, you may say that we cannot change anyone's behavior or attitude, and that is absolutely true. Boundaries, however, are not about the other person.

Boundaries Are for You and About You

WHEN YOU SAY NO TO someone or let someone know that how they are treating you is unacceptable, you are taking care of yourself.

Many people have said to me that when they have set a boundary, the other person will become angry, upset, or even say things to minimize or disparage their opinion. Yes, that happens. Boundaries are *not* about them. Boundaries are a gift you give yourself. We do not have control over how anyone else reacts or behaves; we only have control over how we respond to their behavior. If you are committed to making a change in your life because you are overwhelmed, burdened with responsibility, feeling burnt out, or riddled with the belief that nothing you do is good enough, then setting new and healthy boundaries is an imperative step in changing your life for the better.

Whenever there is a conflict between what you want or need and what someone else wants or needs, one of you may feel upset, hurt, frustrated, disappointed, or angry. *It doesn't always have to be you*, even if you may be used to being the one who always walks away feeling bad or thinking that you just need to suck it up to keep the peace.

When you change this pattern, you will still have feelings of discomfort, but which discomfort you are willing to live with? The old, familiar discomfort of always giving in and feeling frustrated, empty, depressed, exhausted, or powerless, or a new feeling of discomfort because someone else is feeling frustrated or annoyed? And yes, you will think that what you are doing is therefore wrong or bad, but here's an important phrase to remember and rely on: *Setting boundaries is not just about saying no.*

Setting boundaries can also be about making it easier for others to say yes to helping you. Shortly after my husband became disabled and was home all day, every day, I felt a need to be present as much as possible to ease his transition from being an incredibly active man to someone who was so encumbered by pain that he could barely do anything. Something as simple as taking a walk was a challenge for him. I rearranged my schedule so that we could have lunch together most days. I limited my personal activities so that he would not be alone for extended periods of time. This worked fairly well for the first few months, but living a limited existence is hard enough when you don't have a choice. When you do, well, that presents a whole new set of issues and challenges. In my case, I realized that if we were going to handle his being home all the time, we'd have to rework our expectations of ourselves and each other.

Yes, I felt bad about him being alone and feeling isolated. Family and friends were going about their lives and, because Lloyd couldn't participate, many people stopped asking, stopped coming by, stopped checking in. Very few people reached out to see what they could do to help me, so I, as most caregivers do, took on more and more, did more on my own, and didn't think about reaching out to ask for the much desired—if not actually needed—help.

As time went on, it became abundantly clear that while family and friends cared about us, they weren't reaching out to offer assistance because they were immersed in their own lives, stressed for their own reasons, and overwhelmed in their own ways. They didn't know what to do, or what to offer, or what to say. For them, our life's circumstances fell into the background noise of living. As hard as this reality was, this is what happens. People show up for crises, and when the crises pass, everyone's life returns to *their* normal—but the ones living with the now chronic condition and situation have to create a life with a *new* normal. I learned that I had to be the one to ask for what we needed and wanted. I learned this early on, and it's something I share in both my private sessions with individuals and in our Take Back Your Life group program: If you don't ask, the answer is always no. This became a critical life lesson for me. Not only was it about asking for help, it was about identifying *whom* I would ask. It was also an opportunity for my husband to ask for help, support, or just company. Learning to ask when you've spent your life being taught to be independent and self-reliant is a huge challenge.

Setting new boundaries and reaching out to ask for support helped me to learn and grow both professionally and personally. Spending less time in each other's company also helped my husband rethink how he spent his time. He never wanted to be a burden or problem to me or to our children, so he began to encourage activities for each of us. This hadn't been something we discussed at the onset of his disability, primarily because we didn't know at the time how long-term it would be. Individuals can handle most anything for the short term, or in a crisis. But what happens when a disease, illness, or disability becomes chronic and long-term? That's when the real work of self-care comes into sharp focus. Learning to redefine normal is an ongoing life lesson as an individual's disease, abilities, and challenges change, and it's something the "patient" and family need to address openly.

Don't Believe Everything You Think

THOUGHTS OR BELIEFS ARE OFTEN judgments based upon past learning, and what we learned in the past is not necessarily true today. Growing up, you may have been taught to never contradict what your parents said or wanted. Or maybe you learned that you had to give in to what your siblings or friends wanted because you had to share or be "nice." Maybe you learned other rules that prevented you from speaking up and asserting yourself, your feelings, or your needs. Therefore, your thoughts will take you back to those childhood rules. Since setting boundaries, saying no, or taking a stand was not allowed, as soon as you feel the discomfort of doing something differently than you have been, your thoughts or judgments or both will kick in and pull you back to old habits and nothing will change. (Frustrating, right?)

Here's an example of the importance of setting new and healthy boundaries:

Susan's mom, Leslie, who is in assisted living, wanted her to bring some items that she needed from the store: candies that she loved, hand cream, certain snacks that she likes to have in her room—nothing urgent or critical. Leslie insisted that it had to be that day because she was in desperate need. Susan couldn't go that day and knew it wasn't true that it was a desperate situation, *but* she also knew if she said no, her mother would give her a hard time.

"I'm lonely," Leslie said. "You never come to visit me anymore."

"I visit you at least once a week, more when my schedule allows," Susan replied. She has frequently dropped everything and gone to her mother whenever Leslie demanded it. She has rarely denied her mother any request.

"I'm all alone. This place has no good activities, and no one talks to me," Leslie continued. Her list of complaints went on and on.

Susan's anger and frustration grew, and she was about to give in to her mother's demands again just to avoid the inevitable guilt. It didn't matter that she felt put upon and stressed, and was struggling to keep her own life in balance: arranging for someone to take her teenage children to their activities; rearranging her own plans; and putting off preparing a meal for her own family, knowing she'd once again order in dinner instead of having time to cook it herself, and therefore feeling guilty that she was neglecting her own family to take care of her mother. The list in her head was endless. She always felt stuck in a continuous loop of guilt, anger, resentment, and frustration, not to mention the constant feelings of inadequacy on every level.

Fortunately, this time, before Susan responded to her mother's request and before giving in, Susan remembered the lessons she had been learning in our Take Back Your Life: Art of Self-Care group program and took the steps listed below to achieve a different outcome than what she had become used to.

She started with the ever-important question: *What is my desired outcome*? (Remember the two requirements: You must state your answer in terms of what you want, not what you don't want, and it must be something over which you, yourself, have control.)

Susan's goal was to be able to put off going to her mother and deliver the items later in the week when she was already planning to visit.

Remember as you go through these steps that someone might be upset, hurt, angry, or frustrated: It doesn't always have to be you.

1. **And we breathe.** Take a slow, deep breath. This is important because it gives you pause and prevents you from reacting so that you can respond thoughtfully.

2. **Acknowledge** that you have heard the request. In fact, repeat what you have heard. ("I hear mom, that you need your candies, hand-cream, snacks? Is that everything you asked for?")

3. **Validate** that you are aware how important this need is for her. ("I know how much you love having these things available to you when you want.")

4. **Offer an alternative** instead of saying no outright. ("Mom, I wrote down everything that you want and need and I'll be there on Thursday with everything on your list.")

5. **And we breathe.** This step brings you full circle and prevents you from saying anything more because *you have just said no with compassion.*

6. **Compassion:** You will feel a tug, and this step is about maintaining the boundary you have set that is for your greater good. ("Mom, I know that this is difficult for you and I understand your frustration. I'm doing what will work best for my schedule. I appreciate your patience and I'll see you on Thursday.")

If this process seems challenging, I understand. We are talking about making changes that will ultimately enhance and empower your life. All too often we give in to everyone else and cause ourselves many mental, emotional, and physical problems. Setting and maintaining healthy boundaries is a major factor in alleviating these stresses. Boundaries help you to have greater self-esteem and self-respect, to feel greater ease in your life, feel empowered, and connect more fully to feeling loving and loved. Setting boundaries also communicates to yourself and to others that *you matter*. The ability to set and maintain healthy boundaries will greatly improve your overall health and well-being, mentally, emotionally, and physically.

Setting and maintaining healthy boundaries does not mean saying "no" to every request. It means you are able to take as good care of yourself as you do of others in your life. It's important to notice whether, if you say "yes" to someone or something, you are saying "no" to yourself. Setting boundaries means you are aware if you were otherwise undermining or sabotaging yourself in deference to someone else. (I'll discuss self-sabotage in the next chapter).

THROUGHOUT HISTORY, WOMEN HAVE GIVEN selflessly to those they love. We've even ignored or dismissed the idea of self-care, believing that it is an act of selfishness. We may even think it is a sign that we don't love our parents, spouses, children, or friends enough. Here's the truth: *Self-care is not selfishness; it is self-preservation.*

In fact, that is why the lives of most women are so vaguely unsatisfactory. They are always doing secondary and menial things (that do not require all their gifts and ability) for others and never anything for themselves. Society and husbands praise them for it (when they get too miserable or have nervous breakdowns) though always a little perplexedly and half-heartedly and just to be consoling. The poor wives are reminded that that is just why wives are so splendid—because they are so unselfish and self-sacrificing and that is the wonderful thing about them! But inwardly women know that something is wrong. They sense that if you are always doing something for others, like a servant or nurse, and never anything for yourself, you cannot do others any good. You make them physically more comfortable. But you cannot affect them spiritually in any way at all. For to teach, encourage, cheer up, console, amuse, stimulate or advise a husband or children or friends, you have to be something yourself.

—Brenda Ueland, journalist, editor,
freelance writer, and teacher

We all want and need to feel and be appreciated, and all too often caregivers feel taken for granted. Learning to speak up and say what you want, need, and feel changes the dynamics of a relationship. This is not about your ego and needing attention. It is about being valued and appreciated for who you are. When you don't set limits, no one learns that you need and deserve to be acknowledged, appreciated, and respected. In fact, all too often even the medical community (doctors, nurses, and therapists) do not consciously and purposefully pay attention to what is involved in the care of the patient. They do their jobs, and assume everything will be taken care of at home without exploring how and by whom, thus further adding to your stress, overwhelm, and feelings of inadequacy and burn out.

Are you getting the point that, as challenging as it may be to create and maintain healthy boundaries, it is not only necessary, but it really is life-saving. Remember, the commandment that has been around for centuries, "Love thy neighbor as thyself," doesn't say *more than yourself.* As actor, journalist, editor, freelance writer and teacher Edward Albert says, "Sometimes you have to be selfish to be selfless."

You are a loving, caring, compassionate, and amazing individual. You are a caregiver, and these attributes go hand in hand with that role. However, you cannot effectively and lovingly care for someone else if you are not giving yourself enough love, care, affection, time, and energy. Boundaries are not meant to punish, but are for your well-being and protection. They're infinitely more effective when you are assertive, calm, firm, and respectful. Achieving this requires practice, patience and perseverance, and courage. Take one step at a time and know that every time you set even a small boundary, you are one step closer to being able to do so more often and with greater feelings of love, respect, and compassion for yourself and for those you care for.

Many of us follow the commandment "Love One Another." When it relates to caregiving, we must love one another with boundaries. We must acknowledge that we are included in the "Love One Another."

—Peggi Speers, *The Inspired Caregiver*

And we breathe...

Chapter 3 Worksheet

Boundaries: Setting and
Maintaining Healthy Limits

1. What are the signs and signals I feel when my boundaries
   have been crossed, ignored, or violated (physically, mentally,
   or emotionally)?

   _____

   _____

   _____

   _____

2. What have I usually done when my boundaries have been
   disregarded, ignored, or violated (for example, stay silent,
   seethe, act out, withdraw, vent to others)?

   _____

   _____

   _____

   _____

3. What can I do instead? What am I willing to do instead (for
   example, speak up with honesty and compassion for myself)?

   _____

   _____

   _____

   _____

4. If there are behaviors I am no longer willing to accept, how will I take care of myself going forward? What boundaries am I willing to set and maintain?

_____

_____

_____

5. What interferes with my setting of boundaries in any given situation? What am I really afraid of?

_____

_____

_____

6. Is my desired outcome (for example, self-care, self-respect and self-compassion) greater than my fear of others' reactions? If not, what would it take to make my desired outcome stronger?

_____

_____

_____

More Tools for Change: Five Daily Commitments You Must Make to Yourself When Caring for a Family Member

IT'S TIME TO PUT A structure in place that will ensure that you get your own needs met first. That may very well include an attitudinal shift toward giving yourself permission to ask for and receive what you need, no ifs, ands, or buts!

I highly recommend that you add to your morning schedule a daily recitation of the following five declarations. Remind yourself of these as you go through your day:

1. **I remember at all times that my needs count.** I strive to be clear to myself and others about my needs, feelings, and capabilities. This means I put guilt aside and let go of all judgments about those needs. I simply focus on the situation at hand and assess what is required in practical terms. I consider the consequences of possible decisions I could make and actions I could take, including those for myself, my family, my job, finances, and so on. I make no judgments, I simply allow myself to become aware of the true circumstances and my options for responding with respect to everyone's needs including my own.

2. **I ask for the help and support I need and deserve.** I realize there are no "bonus points" I will earn by being a martyr. I realize that, though in the short run my new caregiver role may feel manageable, if the situation becomes a long-term commitment, additional resources must be brought into the mix. I do not have to do, *and do not choose* to do, this loving and exhausting work alone. I identify appropriate human and other support resources and get agreements in advance that I can call on them when and as needed.

3. **I set boundaries that are respectful and realistic.** I acknowledge that I cannot—*and should not!*—attempt to do everything required just because someone expects me

to. Health care professionals may assume that I am prepared to take on all my loved one's care and responsibilities or family members may ask me to do so. However, that doesn't mean I have to say yes. I remind myself, when asked to take on more, to assess the potential for added stress and struggle in my life if I say yes and then make the choice that's right for me; I arrange with someone else to handle that need if that is the appropriate solution.

4. **I schedule regular stress-relieving breaks throughout my day.** Whether I do a twenty-minute meditation, have lunch with a friend, see a movie, watch some funny Internet videos, or take an hourly two-minute meditation break, *I acknowledge that I need and I deserve these regular breaks* to replenish my energies and revitalize myself so I can face the ongoing responsibilities I have taken on.

5. **I am consistently good to myself.** I realize that caring for my loved one involves many changes and adjustments. It's imperative that I be patient, kind, and compassionate to myself, *at all times.* It is not selfish of me to acknowledge that my caregiver role can be stressful and overwhelming. Reducing that stress means making sure *I am taking good care of myself*—physically, emotionally, and every other way. When I think I've made a mistake or fallen short, *I forgive myself quickly.* I pay attention to how I speak to myself and make sure both my words and the underlying messages are kind, compassionate, and understanding.

It may take a while for these commitments to become an automatic part of your day. Since most caregivers do not put themselves on their list of priorities for care, remember that doing so takes practice, patience and perseverance, and courage.

Chapter 4
Preventing Self-Sabotage: Letting Go of Lies Masquerading as Truths

*Chains of habit are too light to be felt
until they are too heavy to be broken.*

—*Warren Buffet*

RECOGNIZING THE IMPORTANCE OF TAKING as good care of yourself as you do of others in your life is critical in moving forward in your life in a positive and meaningful way. Somehow you still seem to get sucked into old patterns, and it seems as if sabotage happens all the time. The question is, why and how does that keep happening?

You set goals, you have desired outcomes, you know what it is you want, yet somehow you find yourself repeating the very behaviors you know undermine and sabotage your successes. You feel frustrated, annoyed, and maybe even a little (or very) guilty, yet you think you have no choice.

Here's what really happens. You set an intention to do something differently. Maybe it's setting a new boundary or limit. Maybe it's speaking up more assertively or asking for help. And then there's a pushback. Someone doesn't like it and they react, sending a message to you that induces feelings of guilt or shame (more about those in a later chapter), and then your feelings awaken certain thoughts and beliefs. These thoughts and beliefs, in turn, trigger unhelpful but familiar behaviors, and these behaviors become your habits. Your habits inevitably bring you to what you know, what is familiar, and what is, therefore, easy. You fall into the same old patterns and continue to berate, judge, and criticize yourself. And there you are in the grip of self-sabotage.

Don't Believe Everything You Think

FEELINGS lead to
THOUGHTS lead to
WORDS lead to
ACTIONS lead to
BEHAVIORS lead to
HABITS lead to
YOUR LIFE

Your feelings are real and they matter. It's your thoughts that bring you back to old habits and beliefs, or can instead offer you a way to *create the possibility* of taking a new route to achieve your desired outcome.

As you begin to break the cycle of self-sabotage, focus on the message: "Don't believe everything you think." Take a moment to let that settle in. What happens if you don't believe everything you think?

Now, this doesn't mean you judge your thoughts as bad or wrong. It simply means you question their veracity. What happens if you question, challenge, and remain skeptical about your very thoughts? What happens in a given moment if you question the habit or behavior you have always practiced and imagine how it might feel to do something new? What could possibly change in your life?

Whether you're going into a situation believing it won't work out for you, or you're going to get screwed royally anyway, or it just doesn't matter what you want or need, when you're stuck in old, unconscious patterns, a part of you is actually driven to behave in some way that will either negate, worsen, undermine, or sabotage something that could otherwise be promising.

Fear of change, as well as fear of dealing with everyone else's negative reactions or judgments, keeps you trapped in the same pattern you have been striving to change and feeling the same frustration and irritation. In many ways, it becomes a "better the devil you know" situation. Even though you know you'll feel bad, you're used to that, and you know you can handle it.

What happens if you actually do things differently? It's scary to step into an unknown, so sometimes there is an unconscious need to keep things the way they are just to avoid feeling scared. But how often do you feel like a victim or martyr? How often do you feel stuck, trapped, or overwhelmed and say, "Nothing will ever work," without even trying to think of alternatives?

Maybe you've reached a point where you believe that suffering, or being at everyone's beck and call, is simply your lot in life. For many caregivers, this habit of knowing how things will go and what others will say or do in the context of caring for Mom or Dad or both gives them the illusion of control. You know what the problem is and you know what the conflicts will be. So even in pain there is that perverse reward.

Sometimes we walk the path of self-sabotage because we don't really feel worthy when our self-esteem hinges on someone else's approval. When you are struggling with caring for somebody who is unappreciative, ungracious, or ungrateful—maybe they are even downright resentful of needing and accepting your help—it triggers feelings of being unworthy and inadequate. About yourself and the situation, or both, you may think, *I can never get anything right!* or, *It doesn't really matter what I do; it's never enough and it never ends.* It's a very painful loop when you're stuck in the belief that nothing will ever change. When you are stuck feeling unworthy, you are certain to find yourself following old habits and falling into the same traps.

How many times have you used busyness, or even addictive behavior, to cover up feeling inadequate, feeling *not good enough?* Are you smoking, drinking, overeating, undereating, constantly on the go, struggling with overwhelming busyness? How are you punishing yourself in that loop of *nothing ever works?*

How many times have you heard yourself say, "Maybe next time will be different," or, "Maybe next time they'll see how much I do, or, If I can just make them see," in your role as caregiver?

The Five Basic Forms Self-Sabotage Usually Takes

1. **The familiarity of failure:** *It'll never work,* and you're just used to that.
2. **The illusion of being in control:** You know what is going to happen if you do something and you live with the illusion, *I got this.*

3. **Chasing appreciation and recognition:** You feel unworthy and always hope that *Someday they'll appreciate and recognize all I do for them.*

4. **Martyrdom:** You use this as an excuse for addictive, self-destructive behaviors, and it contributes to self-pity and feeling powerless to make changes.

5. **Drama:** You always have a story to tell, a problem to solve, a challenge to overcome, and chaos which prevents dealing with life outside of caregiving.

If you are used to any of these scenarios, think about how that makes you feel. Don't form negative judgments, seek awareness and clarity. For example, if you feel like a martyr and people who know about your struggles feel sorry for you, think about what that means to you. Maybe they reach out to you with sympathy and, while that may not make the situation any better, you feel validated. You believe you matter, and on some level this feels comforting enough that you are motivated to keep seeking that response from others. And so the cycle of falling into the same painful pattern perpetuates.

When you don't make conscious choices you end up repeating patterns. You cannot control what anyone else will say or do when they need your help, need care, or need your services. Neither can you control anyone else's reaction to your choice to handle situations differently than they are used to. However, you can choose, each and every time, how you want to handle these moments. This is where the shift comes in—the shift to choose to take a deep breath and take a new turn in this road of life, called "What's your desired outcome?" When your goal—your desired outcome—is stronger and more important than your fear of the repercussions when you make a change, you will move forward. Use the Caregiver's Step-by-Step Guide to take it even further and speed up your results. (Download at www.lorenGelbergGoff.com/sbsg-tbyl or see Appendix 1.)

As scary as it is to make changes and to face the backlash that can bring, change really is inevitable. Whether change happens at different times in your life because you actively choose to do things differently or due to circumstances beyond your control (a shift in needs, medical conditions, or demands), you have to deal with the concept of behaving differently than you're used to.

While you may feel isolated and disconnected in your dilemmas and challenges, you are not alone. More than forty-three million people in the United States alone are providing care for a family member. That's potential for a huge support system, and support does exist, even if you are not yet aware of all the forms it can take.

I started the Take Back Your Life support group for caregivers because, in order to change self-sabotaging behaviors, you are going to have to feel and tolerate some uncertainty and doubt and perhaps even fear and anxiety. It helps immensely to have an experienced guide who is not only trained in helping to deal with making big changes, but also has walked the walk herself. It is also a huge help to be among a group of fellow travelers on the path to creating a life beyond just being a caregiver. And because it's virtual (we meet via telephone conference calls and use online educational tools), anyone can be a part of the group no matter where they live on the planet. Thank goodness for technology!

Whether you go it alone or have a support system, *you are going to have some uncomfortable feelings as you make these changes.* There's just no way around it. You will probably experience some stress and tension, because you are challenging deeply ingrained, old, and familiar attitudes that you've held about yourself, including attitudes and beliefs that your parents and family members held about you. These created habits for you, such as those that keep you doing the same things and hoping that this time it will work out better. Having support, guidance, and encouragement to implement these new self-care attitudes and behaviors makes a huge difference, and high-impact groups are particularly successful at helping you to do that.

It's time to ask yourself: *Do I deserve to feel happy, fulfilled, content, and at ease with myself—right now?* If the answer is "yes!" then know that you don't have to wait for someone to get healthy, pass on, or move away in order to feel good about your life. Your willingness to feel good, whole, and empowered within yourself does not have to be contingent on someone else's behavior, attitude, or beliefs.

What would be different for you if you could take care of your needs and feelings with compassion and respect, even if others in your life do not support or encourage this change in your approach to life? Shifting perspectives on a given situation can also help you to move forward in a new direction, in spite of doubt and resistance within yourself or from others. When you are willing to challenge your thoughts and beliefs and question their validity, new options open up to you.

Karen's Story

HERE IS AN EXAMPLE OF a caregiver who came to realize she could have more say in her day-to-day experience without having to abandon caring for her loved one to do so.

A number of years ago Karen was caring for her mother, who lived alone. While Karen's mother had some health problems, her primary issue was depression about getting old. She refused to leave her apartment, didn't want to do anything on her own, and wanted only to be cared for by her daughter. Karen was married, had two children, and worked full-time. Yet Karen went to help her mother almost daily. She shopped, cooked, cleaned, did her mother's laundry, helped her mother bathe, and handled her mother's bills. Needless to say, this was like having a second full-time job.

By the time Karen decided to get help and began working with me, the pattern had continued for a number of years. Karen didn't enjoy her responsibilities to her mother and resented that her siblings never stepped in to help.

"They all have excuses," Karen explained to me. "If I didn't do everything, nothing would get done, and my mother would suffer."

At first, Karen wasn't willing to look at other options, such as hiring a home health aide, assigning some responsibilities to her siblings, or having groceries delivered. "My mother would never agree," Karen always said.

So Karen was exhausted and rapidly burning out. She powered on like this until she was told that she, herself, needed surgery that would put her out of commission for about six weeks. This forced her to explore options that before this new event were unthinkable and seemed undoable.

As I said, change happens whether we want it to or not. Karen's upcoming surgery obligated her to make changes in both her beliefs and her behaviors. Even though she believed that her mother would not accept care from anyone but her, Karen hired an aide who took on cooking and cleaning for her mom, doing the laundry, bathing her mom, and handling general daily care. Lo and behold, it turned out that Karen's mother actually thrived under this attention. Karen also began ordering her mother's groceries online and having them delivered; Karen continued to manage her mother's finances and pay her bills. During her recuperation, Karen's siblings visited their mother and began showing up more often, giving Karen much-needed time with her family and friends. She was really liking this new arrangement, which she had resisted for so long.

During her session with me after she recuperated from her surgery, Karen seemed lighter, somehow. She smiled easily and seemed at ease. "I realized I don't want to go back to the way it was. I don't want to have all of the care and responsibilities for my mother."

So you can see how, for years, in spite of doing what she didn't want to do and believing there was no other option, Karen had resisted making any changes in her mom's care *for fear of upsetting her mother* and possibly causing an increase in her depression. Yet because Karen had no choice but to take time off, her siblings suddenly stopped making excuses for why they couldn't help out. They showed up! Yes, they were annoyed initially, not because Karen needed surgery or couldn't do everything she had been doing, but because their lives would now have to be amended in some way. As we all do when life takes an unexpected turn, they adjusted and adapted (*and we breathe*).

So the question is, how might Karen have tapped into this array of care resources and her siblings' ability to help out without waiting until she was sidelined by a medical condition that took her temporarily offline? That's exactly the question that a high-impact support group can help you answer.

Are you willing to challenge long-held beliefs about yourself and your family? Are you willing to make new decisions that fly in the face of family traditions and family beliefs? For example, if the person you care for told you they could never accept help at home from a hired caregiver, because "no one will do the work, or help me the way you do," then you may have to stand your ground about a decision to make a change. And whether you hire a professional caregiver to help or allow other family members to step in, owning a new boundary brings new possibilities into your life that were beyond your reach while you were powering on in autopilot mode.

Karen discovered that she could pay attention to her own life. She was even able to go away on a much-needed vacation with her family. It had been years since they went away for even a weekend. Who knows what may be possible for you, once you open up your perspective?

Are you willing to separate from those negative, self-destructive behaviors and beliefs that cause you to sabotage what it is you really want, need, and deserve in your life? In other words, are you willing to question your thoughts and beliefs? Are you willing to explore a new path for living your life?

Are you willing to look at your values, your goals, and your beliefs and decide—for the first time, perhaps—what you really and truly want them to be? To give them due credit, your old beliefs have done *one thing* for you in the past: They helped you survive. So we are not judging any old habit, any behavior or belief, because they have all served a purpose in your life. On the other hand, you're reading this book now because something isn't working for you anymore. You have reached out to claim an opportunity to make a change and you're ready to question those beliefs, as well as the habits and behaviors the beliefs have kept in place up until now.

While I'm at it, I want to acknowledge that all behaviors serve a purpose. A behavior may have been very functional growing up. Doing whatever was asked without question, or hiding under your covers whenever you got scared, overwhelmed, or upset, may have helped you feel very safe and be successful when those behaviors were first learned, but are they still helpful now that you are an adult? It may have been acceptable to give in to everyone when you were growing up and to have everybody say about you, "Oh, she's such a good person, she's so nice, and she never complains. She's so easy to get along with." Maybe it was important back then to have approval, so that behavior worked really well for you. But is being "nice," while ignoring your own needs and feelings, benefiting you today? Is it enhancing or empowering your life today? If not, it's time to trade up to more empowering behaviors.

Your internal voice wants to pull you back into behaviors it knows. That's where taking a deep breath comes in. You *stop*. You *breathe*. You *focus*: *What is my desired outcome?* Your old thoughts and long-held beliefs often hold you back from getting what you really want. Considering making changes can trigger fears within you that you'll be hurt in some way; you might be rejected, demeaned, dismissed, or punished. The idea of changing may trigger fear that someone else in your life—your parent, spouse, or children—will be hurt by your changes. You may fear that they'll feel angry, disappointed, upset, or neglected, and that sets you in motion once again to respond in the old way that you know so well.

It's time now to change direction, to breathe through the old beliefs and those old fears. In many cases, an old belief is that your needs and feelings don't really matter or that someone else's needs and feelings matter more. It may be the belief that somehow it's okay if you feel bad, but it's not okay if someone else does when it's within your power to prevent that from happening by sacrificing yourself. Taking a deep breath helps you shift to thinking that you are, in fact, allowed to take as good care of yourself as you do of the others in your life.

> *MY NEEDS AND FEELINGS*
> *are as important to me*
> *as your needs and feelings*
> *are to you.*

By becoming aware of what your habits and patterns are and recognizing them—not judging them, but being aware—and then taking that breath, you can start to look at what pulls you back into habits and behaviors that really don't feel good, but do feel familiar and therefore known and managed. With awareness, you can take the first step to avoid sabotaging yourself and your relationships and actually provide more loving and compassionate care to those you love.

Please be patient with yourself. Making changes requires courage to take that first step in a new direction. Then comes practice, patience, and perseverance. You have to keep your desired outcome in mind. And as long as your desired outcome is stronger than your fear, you will move forward and make changes to end self-sabotage.

As you look at the workbook pages at the end of each chapter, give yourself time to do the work. Really weed out: What really doesn't work for you today, even though it seems normal? Just because something feels normal doesn't mean it feels good and doesn't mean it is healthy for you mentally, emotionally, or physically.

When you are willing to take responsibility for your life, you are no longer a victim. Even as a caregiver who says, "But there's nobody else who can take care of my mother, there's nobody else who can take care of my father, it's all on me," take a breath and explore some of the resources that may be open to you.

Beliefs: Truth or Lies?

> *Beliefs dictate your life as surely as magnetism*
> *directs a compass needle. If you deem yourself*
> *unworthy, you'll prove it to be so.*
> *If you think you're unfit, you'll find a way to*
> *manifest that. I cannot overemphasize both the*

*potential power in our beliefs and the necessity of
choosing them wisely.*

—*Eldon Taylor,* I Believe: When What
You Believe Matters

Be sure to look at the buy-in you give to your beliefs. It's not your thoughts that drive you; it's your beliefs. When you find yourself repeating patterns and behaviors that really don't support and empower you, stop and think about what belief brought you there. Remember, the first and most important step in preventing self-sabotage is being conscious and aware of your thoughts, your beliefs, and your habits. It's through awareness that you can then explore a desired outcome and begin to shift gears. *Value who you are, as you are, and know that who you are is enough.* Everything you do, everything you give, everything you share, that's icing on the cake.

As you go through the chapters to come, you will discover that change is about letting go of lies masquerading as truths. This is a step-by-step learning process of acquiring the skills for taking as good care of yourself as you do of others in your life. Remember the analogy of airplane travel and place the oxygen mask over your face first. Because if you're not breathing (that is, taking care of yourself), you won't be able to take care of anybody else.

BEFORE YOU MOVE ON TO the workbook pages for this chapter, think about and practice the following exercise in preventing burnout and self-sabotage:

1. Think about the fact that you are energy, and everything around you is energy. We give out energy from the right side and we take in energy on our left side. As you read this, open your right hand and think about all the energy you give out to those in your life. Are you giving love, time, attention, compassion, energy, patience, and understanding? Feel all that energy going out into the world, into the people you care about the most.

2. Now, open your left hand, and feel what energy you're taking in through your experiences in your life. What's coming in? Stress? Responsibility? Obligation? Aggravation? Overwhelm? How much love, affection, respect, and compassion are you receiving?

3. Consider: Is there a balance between the two sides? Or, are things significantly unbalanced, in that you are giving out so much more good than you are taking in? You are not an alchemist. You cannot turn stress, aggravation, and exhaustion into love.

It's important to see both sides. What are you doing to replenish your energy, your love, and your resilience? What are you doing to replenish these treasures within you so that you can lovingly, compassionately, understandingly, and patiently give to the people in your life?

If giving and receiving within you are not balanced, then it's no wonder you feel depleted, burnt out, and fatigued. It's imperative that you start doing things to replenish and revitalize your energy.

Examine what you believe you deserve. If you live with the belief that you don't deserve much, or that you are not worthy unless you are giving until it hurts, work on changing this belief to one that is healthier for you.

You must be sure to take time for yourself, whether it's reading a book, putting your feet up, or taking a nap. (By the way, I am a huge fan and advocate of taking a power nap every day. That is one of the ways I replenish my own energy.) Maybe there is a sport you like to participate in or to watch. Do you have a guilty pleasure for which you have not made time in quite a while? Make a list of things you could do, or would love to give yourself permission to do, that could replenish and recharge your batteries.

Think about what you need or would like that replenishes your energy. If you're going to stop the cycle of self-sabotage, you first have to know and embrace the reality that you're worth taking care of, first and foremost.

And we breathe...

Chapter 4 Worksheet

Preventing Self-Sabotage: Letting Go of Lies Masquerading as Truths

1. Feelings trigger thoughts and beliefs. Where in my body do I first experience my feelings? Do they hit my stomach, heart, chest, neck/shoulders, throat, hands?

   _____

   _____

   a. What is the initial thought that gets triggered by this emotion?

      _____

      _____

      _____

   b. What is the belief that underscores this thought?

      _____

      _____

      _____

2. What did this belief do for me in the past (for example, kept me safe, kept the peace, maintained a "don't rock the boat" status quo)?

   _____

   _____

   _____

3. What does this belief do for me today?

_____

_____

4. Is it a belief I still need or want?

_____

_____

5. Does this belief move me forward toward my goal to take as good care of myself as I do of the others in my life? _____ If the answer is no, what new belief am I willing to bring into my life? What new possibilities for my life can I explore?

_____

_____

_____

_____

More Tools for Change: Affirmation for Reframing Negative Thoughts

As CAREGIVERS, WE OFTEN LET negative thoughts interfere with the quality of our lives. Over time, these thoughts can lead to creating limiting beliefs. You may recognize some of these thoughts as your own:

- "I can never get anything right!"
- "I'm going to get screwed royally, anyway."
- "This will never work."
- "Nothing ever works."

- "It doesn't really matter what I do; it's never enough and it never ends."
- "I'm not good enough."
- "Maybe next time will be different."
- "Maybe next time they'll see how much I do."

Instead of focusing on what hasn't worked or what you fear will never change, focus on the following affirmation as you bring changes into your life:

I allow myself the possibility and opportunity to practice new beliefs and new behaviors that reflect a positive and empowered perspective about myself and my worth.

Chapter 5
Anger and Resentment:
The Obstacles and the Gifts

Learn this from me: holding anger is a poison.
It eats you from inside. We think that hating is a
weapon that attacks the person who harmed us,
but hatred is a curved blade, and the harm
we do we do to ourselves.

—*Mitch Albom,* The Five People
You Meet in Heaven

STEPPING UP TO HANDLE LIFE's challenges became part and parcel of my life as my husband's disability extended year after year. Early on it was easy to handle daily responsibilities and, in fact, I felt very proud of myself for all I could manage between our children's schedules, my practice, and my husband's doctor visits, tests, and therapies.

It all seemed to be okay until the afternoon he was scheduled for an EMG. When we arrived at the doctor's office, my husband asked, "Where are my x-rays?"

"You didn't bring them?" I asked.

"I thought you brought them," he replied.

While the office was only fifteen minutes away from home, I knew that I would have to be the one to return home to retrieve the forgotten x-rays. This could potentially delay his appointment, thus throwing my schedule off completely. I was pissed! I took a deep breath and walked purposefully (and maybe even dramatically) out of the office to our car.

The entire way home I ranted and raved at the empty seat beside me. "I'm so angry! You are so frustrating. Why didn't you tell me you needed your x-rays? Why didn't you remember to bring them? Why is everything always on me? I am exhausted and I have no help!"

The empty seat beside me listened patiently to my tirade and was waiting for me when I jumped back in the car with the x-rays in hand. I continued my rant for most of my return trip, finally recognizing that neither of us had communicated very well with each other about the requirements for this appointment. He had grown used to my handling and remembering everything, and I still wanted him to take responsibility for things he clearly struggled to remember. (His medications really messed with his memory.)

By the time I reached the doctor's office I felt calmer, quieter, and less hostile and knew I had hit a turning point in my caregiving. I was in a better position to communicate my feelings and provide care, love, and support without resentment and knew I had created a new kind of balance in our relationship.

I was able to tell Lloyd in a calm, clear voice, "Going forward, we need to write down requirements for appointments and leave them as notes by the front door so we can confirm we have whatever is needed before leaving the house." My being able to freely rant, yell, and lash out without anyone being hurt by it reinforced what I had always known professionally. Now I felt the impact of this truth: Anger needs a voice. As Julia Cameron remarked in *The Artist's Way,* "Anger is meant to be acted upon. It is not meant to be acted out."

In this chapter, we start with the question of what happened when you became a caregiver. If you've been doing this for a long time, you may feel anger, resentment, hurt, and a strong sense of being overwhelmed. The two obvious questions to ask are, Why do these feelings keep coming up? And what do you do with them?

Anger and resentment tend to trigger a lot of guilt and shame, because the person you're caring for is in need, and we're taught to be compassionate and helpful. So isn't it selfish and wrong to become angry or resentful about caring for someone in need?

Anger, especially, brings up a whole host of challenges. I want to start by sharing some more messages from Julia Cameron's book *The Artist's Way,* as she so beautifully expresses the foundation from which we will explore this topic:

> Anger is meant to be listened to. Anger is a voice, a shout, a plea, a demand. Anger is meant to be respected. Why? Because anger is a map. Anger shows us what our boundaries are. Anger shows us where we want to go. It lets us see where we've been and lets us know when we haven't liked it.
>
> Anger is meant to be acted upon. It is not meant to be acted out. Sloth, apathy and despair are the enemy. Anger is not. Anger is our friend. Not a nice friend, not a gentle friend, but a very, very, loyal friend. It will always tell us when we have been betrayed. It will always tell us when we have betrayed ourselves. It will always tell us it is time to act in our own best interest.

Let's start from the premise, which is unusual for many people to consider, that anger is our friend. We all have different reactions to anger. We've all grown up with different messages about what anger is. Maybe you were told as a child, "Don't be angry. Let it go. Forget about it." When we get messages like that, we learn to believe that anger is a bad thing.

Many people have also experienced anger in a very negative way. When you were growing up and your parents were angry with you, chances are you did not feel their love. Think about how people look when they're angry. They don't look loving and they certainly don't sound loving. Faces are scrunched up, eyes flash, and voices are raised, sounding scary; often threatening words are used to further frighten and intimidate you. When someone is angry with you, even today, you are probably not feeling their love. When you're angry with someone, chances are you don't feel very loving either. In those moments of anger, love for that person seems to disappear.

From these experiences, we create internal beliefs that undermine and sabotage our relationship with anger. While it is true that intimacy and anger cannot coexist, not within yourself and not within your other relationships, it is only true when anger is unchecked and unaddressed in a meaningful and productive way. This is why we start with the message from Julia Cameron that "anger is your friend." This is about learning new ways of experiencing and dealing with your anger.

Express Your Anger

ANGER SERVES A PURPOSE. ITS purpose is to release deeper issues, problems, and internal conflict. It's a built-in pressure-release valve for human beings that actually serves you well. From your body's perspective, it's better to release anger than to turn it around to destroy yourself.

You may be familiar with one of the basic premises of depression, that it is anger that you turn inward, that you use against yourself. We need to find a way to productively and effectively experience, deal with, and communicate our angry feelings.

Let's start with understanding the basics of anger. Anger is an emotional response to a perceived injustice. Anger is energy. It moves you toward action. Then you have to determine if that action is for your greater good, or exactly the opposite, as can sometimes be the case.

Strike while the iron is hot may work well in certain situations. However, it is not one I recommend when dealing with anger or any other intense emotion. In these circumstances, it's best to let cooler heads prevail. Remember Julia Cameron's words: "Anger is meant to be acted upon. It is not meant to be acted out." Brené Brown, research professor at the University of Houston, author, and speaker on the topic of shame and vulnerability, has a rule when it comes to feeling angry. When in a state of anger, Dr. Brown says, "do not talk, text or type."

So when you feel angry, become aware of where in your body you first feel that anger. For some people it's in the pit of their stomach; for others it's in their chest. Some people feel that their face and head get red hot and their ears burn. Wherever it is for you, *that's your instantaneous cue* that you have some anger to process, before it takes over and you react without thinking.

When emotions take over, intellect walks out, and you get caught in a loop of acting out your anger—doing or saying something you'll regret later, feeling guilty about it, making amends and then starting the cycle all over again—unless you are willing to *Stop! Breathe! Focus!* Breathe through your urge to lash out or implode. Wait until you can have a clear, desired outcome that will feel productive and meaningful. Again, "Anger shows us where we want to go," and "Anger is meant to be respected." It is really not meant to be released on or at anyone, including yourself; it is an alert for you that something is wrong.

Once you become aware of the signal that tells you you're feeling angry, breathe and allow yourself to acknowledge, respect, and accept your feelings. You don't have to do anything with them. As you will read many times throughout this book, it is not your feelings that get you into trouble; it is your actions.

There are four ways in which anger can be expressed:

1. **Imploding**: Keeping anger in can result in hypertension, gastric problems, and depression.
2. **Exploding**: Lashing out can be hostility or aggression, causing potential fights, and damage to self or others.
3. **Passive aggression**: Getting back at someone indirectly; being sarcastic, cynical, or hostile without communicating clearly and directly what you are reacting to.
4. **Calming down internally**: Understanding and processing your feelings so that you can clearly and directly address the issue at hand with rational thought and words.

When you suppress anger it becomes self-destructive. The negative energy gets redirected into your body, and anger then becomes a path to destruction. Anger's purpose is to alert you to problems. You can use this alert to address and work through the issue, but that will only happen when you are communicating in an effective and productive way. Otherwise anger will just create more problems.

If you lash out in anger, you end up attracting anger, hostility, passive aggression or your own implosions. Will you stoop to a lower level or look for ways to take the high road? Taking the high road does not mean you avoid, ignore, or deny a problem. It simply means you choose to handle the problem with a clear, direct, and productive desired outcome.

Sam's Story

SAM'S PARENTS WERE AGING, AND their physical abilities were declining. They continually told him that they could manage on their own and didn't want or need help at home. After all, they had each other and they took care of each other. They cooked, cleaned, went out, and, against Sam's better judgment, they were still driving. As independent as they claimed to be, Sam received daily calls about something else that went wrong or something they needed, and everything seemed to be an emergency.

Sam felt increasingly frustrated and annoyed as the weeks went on. He spoke with his sister, who also lived nearby. However, she had a job that required a great deal of travel. She wasn't around as often, so she was spared the numerous phone calls and the ongoing arguments Sam had with his parents.

Sam would leave work early on many days to run errands for his parents, with the hope that it would prevent them from driving. He would beg them to attend a senior center during the day so that they would have a social outlet other than each other. He implored them to get help at home. They rejected everything, saying that they loved having him come and visit and they were afraid that if they did all that he asked, he'd stop visiting. They did not see that Sam didn't feel like he was visiting; he was caregiving, and on constant alert. He knew they were not on the same page, and his frustration, resentment, and anger were growing day by day and call by call.

Sam became increasingly irritable at home and at work. He told me, "People at work have been mentioning my short temper. I can't help it—every little thing sets me off. I can't sleep. I'm exhausted all the time."

Sam was visibly drained and on edge. He seemed to be at his wit's end, and his behavior confirmed that. "I tried yelling at my parents. I know it was wrong, but I was hoping that, if they heard how I angry I was, they would change." Sam sighed. "Of course, after the screaming match I felt horrible. So much guilt. I wish I hadn't yelled at them. They're so frail, and I have to be kind to them—no matter what."

Sam had nowhere to go with his feelings, so he became even more depressed and frustrated. At one point, Sam decided that he just wouldn't take his parents' calls. He started ordering their groceries online and having them delivered as a way to prevent them from driving to the store. He sent home health aides to their home without telling them, with the hope that they wouldn't do anything to cause themselves injuries. His parents didn't let the aides in and they didn't take kindly to having groceries that they hadn't chosen show up at their doorstep.

Sam went through the gamut of reactions to his anger and saw that he wasn't getting the results he wanted, which was to keep his parents safe, enjoy visiting with them, and be able concentrate at work and relax at home. His anger got in the way. As I stated before, intimacy and anger cannot coexist. As long as Sam was being ruled by his anger and frustration, he was stuck.

Sam had to take a breath. He had to face his anger and accept how he was feeling. Feelings are never wrong—they just are. He had to find a new way to address and deal with his feelings of anger, frustration, and resentment. Sam began to realize that much of his anger was because he felt powerless and helpless when dealing with his parents. He had to work on new boundaries and change how he responded to their daily requests. He had to acknowledge what he needed, not just what they needed. This did not mean that Sam lost his compassion for his parents and their declining independence and abilities. It meant that when he could connect to compassion for himself, he would be better able to address his parents' situation and needs.

Anger is there for a reason. It's alerting you to something that requires your attention. Aa Julia Cameron writes in *The Artist's Way*, "[Anger] will always tell us when we have been betrayed. It will always tell us when we have betrayed ourselves. It will always tell us it is time to act in our own best interest."

After taking time to breathe and address his feelings, Sam gained clarity about his own actions. "I see now that going behind my parents' backs to get them the services they need backfired, he said. I've decided that I need to go with them to their doctor's appointments so that the conversation about them driving can be with all of us and not just me begging them."

This proved to be a good decision. The doctor was able to confirm that Sam's parents should not be driving, and the conversation then moved on to their changing and declining abilities, loss of independence, and fears of isolation and deprivation. These were serious issues for sure, and ones that could now be more openly addressed between Sam, his parents, and his sister.

Changing how Sam dealt with his feelings of resentment, frustration, and anger opened up new possibilities for different outcomes. It didn't change the situation he faced, but it did change how the situation could be addressed and handled. This one conversation did not eliminate Sam's anger, but it opened him up to all the other feelings his anger had overshadowed, including sadness, fear, upset, and loss.

Sam was consumed with one feeling, and it prevented him from seeing other options and possibilities for handling everything with his parents. Once he was able to open up, first with me, and then with his parents' doctor, he no longer felt as helpless and powerless. This became a huge turning point in coping more authentically with his parents. He began working more closely with his sister to better understand and address his parents' fears and concerns as their abilities declined and their needs increased.

Most problems can be resolved, managed, and coped with more effectively when you are able to process your feelings and gain clarity on your desired outcome(s). Turn to your Caregiver's Step-by-Step Guide so you can focus on new options for handling the issues that come up. (Download at www.lorenGelbergGoff.com/sbsg-tbyl or see Appendix 1.) You do not have to stay stuck with excuses, rationalizations, or apologies. You go straight to what is most likely to actually be helpful: asking yourself, *What's my desired outcome?*

If you have acted out in anger and you need to apologize, do so once, make amends, and move on quickly. If it's something that you feel guilty about, and it is triggering your anger, we'll deal with forgiveness in Chapter 7. For now, take a deep breath and respect how you feel and that you are learning to manage your challenging feelings in new, healthier, and more effective ways.

We're not changing the past; we're learning from it. If it's a situation that really cannot be resolved right away, understand that making changes in how you cope with your challenging feelings is a process, and remember, it takes *courage, practice, patience, and perseverance.* Don't give up on yourself!

The "Never-minds"

CAREGIVERS OFTEN DO NOT ACKNOWLEDGE any anger until it's an explosion or a major implosion. If you hear yourself saying or thinking things like, *It doesn't matter, She can't help it, It's all right, Who cares, Someday it will be better,* or, *Never mind,* you may be pushing aside feelings and issues. If you find yourself saying things like that throughout the day, and throughout the week, allow yourself to *Stop! Breathe! Focus!*

What is that little twinge you're saying "Never mind" about? Those little never-minds build up. And you eventually get to a point where your anger suddenly feels overwhelming—either externally, and you have an explosion, or internally, and you suffer all the consequences of your unexpressed anger.

In situations like this, we're either going to explode, implode, or find a way to be passive-aggressive. These attitudes and behaviors manifest in behaving as a bully, a victim, or a martyr, none of whom are happy people. We're working on achieving the internally calming strategy. Counselors have long said, "You have to feel it to heal it. A feeling denied is intensified."

This book is really about healing for yourself, taking care of yourself through these feelings, so that you are not holding things in and sabotaging your life.

The workbook pages at the end of this chapter will help you become aware of what you do with your angry and resentful feelings. Do you implode and become depressed? Do you explode? Do you have anger management issues that interfere with your relationships—not only with the person you're caring for, but with other people in your life? Remember: Unresolved anger cannot coexist with intimacy.

The "ART" of Coping with Anger

DEALING WITH ANGER BY FEELING it and finding healthy ways to voice it is an "ART." It requires Acceptance, Respect, and Time. It's very important to remember that "acceptance" doesn't mean "like." We can accept our feelings—it doesn't mean we like them, and it doesn't mean they feel good. If you are struggling with this issue, please reach out. Support and guidance are available; check out Appendix 2 at the end of this book.

You may not like freezing cold weather, but you accept it, staying in where it's warm and dressing appropriately when you have to go outside. You may not like it, but you accept it. You have to—it's a reality. And you know it's something you have to deal with. Well, feelings are the same thing. We must accept what we feel.

When we do not respect our feelings and refuse to deal with our anger, when we do our best to push our feelings aside and say they don't matter, a number of issues come up. When we push our anger aside, when we suppress it or deny it, we end up walking around with guilt, shame, and humiliation. We can even suffer health consequences, such as high blood pressure, headaches, and gastric problems as well as fatigue; some people even suffer from rashes, skin irritation, twitches, and anxiety, to name just a few.

Time is necessary because not everything can be addressed and handled immediately. You need time to process your feelings and determine your desired outcome and how you want to present it, or find options to better deal with the issue that is causing you distress.

Coping with Anger is an **ART**:

Acknowledge it
Respect it
Take **T**ime to process it

Often when people feel angry, they look for reasons to justify it. You want validation because people want to be right. You want to know that what you're feeling is justified. You deserve to have your feelings validated because feelings are not wrong. It's how you deal with them that may be problematic. *It's not your feelings that get you into trouble, it's your actions.* The goal here is help you discover new, more effective ways to communicate and express what you feel.

When anger isn't expressed, your heart rate and blood pressure rise, stomach acid builds up, and you may go into a reaction of fight (lash out and become aggressive) or flight (run away). Or you might freeze (avoidance).

Whether you have a fight, flight, or freeze reaction, your adrenaline kicks in, cortisol is released, your breathing rate increases, and your muscles tighten. As your body revs up, when there is no resolution, when there is no solution, anger becomes chronic. And that's when it leads to ongoing mental, emotional, and physical health problems.

So let's explore what you can do if you recognize that anger is a real issue for you. What sets you off? What is the trigger that sends bolts of anger through you? You may have a few, you may have many, or you may have only one. It's okay! There isn't any judgment of how angry you feel. This is about becoming aware of what triggers your anger. Remember what Julia Cameron stated: "Anger is your friend. It's your alarm system. It lets you know something is wrong."

What sets the alarm bells off in you? Is it an old belief? Remember when we were talking about beliefs that are lies masquerading as truths? Just be aware. Is it a problem that can be resolved? Maybe you haven't thought about another way of handling a situation that keeps showing up. Turn to your Caregiver's Step-by-Step Guide. You can explore what new options you might have for handling this issue, problem, or obstacle. Is your anger a result of guilt? Is your anger a result of feeling blackmailed or manipulated? If and when you do express your anger, how do you express it?

These questions, and this process, all move you in the direction of healthy communication. And in case you want to explore creating a real-time support system for yourself, as you start making these discoveries and shifts, you can find a link in Appendix 2 for the support group where we go through this process together over several months, with weekly guidance and feedback. Self-awareness and healthy communication are vitally important and essential, as they have an impact on how we handle and cope with anger.

Carla's Story

ANGER IS A PARTICULARLY SENSITIVE issue for many caregivers, because as caregivers you've been taught to care more about the person you're caring for, and others in your life, than about yourself. You've absorbed the idea that it's not okay to feel angry with someone who is in need of care.

Carla is taking care of her mother, who is not accepting of her need for help, and therefore doesn't receive the care Carla provides with gratitude and appreciation. She's angry that she can't be totally independent anymore. So when Carla comes to help, her mother gets angry with her and complains to her about all the problems and obstacles she faces every day. If only Carla did things when she asked or did them well, none of these problems would exist. She tells Carla both overtly and through her attitude that Carla never does anything right, messes everything up, and never does enough for her.

For a long time, Carla silently took in her mother's hostility, negative comments, and hurtful messages and kept thinking, *Well,*

I feel bad for her. It's a shame that she has to live this way and it's not like she was always like this. She was a good mother, so I can deal with this.

Carla wasn't consciously aware of the pain she herself was feeling at being spoken to in that way by her mother while she was giving so generously of her love, her time, her energy, and her attention while simultaneously managing a household, holding down a full-time job, and doing volunteer work for her children's school.

Through it all, she just kept going, enduring her mother's criticisms, and saying to herself, *It doesn't matter.* Then one day she woke up with a severe migraine and couldn't visit her mother. The migraine kept her in bed, and her mother called and yelled at her, saying things like, "You're supposed to be here! How come you're not here? What's the matter with you?"

There was no compassion and no understanding. And Carla lashed out at her and said, "You don't give a damn about me, and yet I come all the time to help you. You just don't give a damn about me!" She slammed the phone down, then spent days feeling guilty about it.

When Carla connected to the Take Back Your Life group program, she learned that she could set new boundaries with her mother. She listened to the group calls and sent me questions and concerns by email or voicemail. Carla was not comfortable sharing her thoughts, challenges, and feelings out loud, but she loved the idea of having support and guidance for making changes in her life. Carla learned that while it was okay for her mother to feel angry and resentful, it was not okay for her mother to lash out at her. She also learned that her own lashing out was not productive. She finally accepted that it was both understandable and acceptable to feel angry. It's okay to express your anger in a productive way. It is not okay to dump on anyone else. Remember what Julia Cameron wrote, that "...anger is to be acted on, not acted out."

When you are expressing yourself in anger and the target is someone else, you're either blaming them, finding fault with them, or demanding that they change. This tends to be an exercise in futility.

If you've ever taken care of a baby who has thrown up on you, the first thing you do is clean them up, wash them, and clean yourself up—and then you hug them. When someone is turning their anger on you by verbally dumping (vomiting) on you, you are not going to feel that loving, warm, fuzzy feeling that has you wanting to hug and embrace them. You are going to want to get out of the way of the onslaught.

Instead of yelling back or becoming hostile in some way, simply step back, step away, and breathe. Let their anger go by, like watching a river flow downstream. Do not react. If someone is verbally dumping on you, I liken it to someone having a tantrum. It's important *not* to engage with someone having a tantrum. We must let the tantrum pass before any meaningful dialogue can occur. What if you're the one having that tantrum? If you're feeling like you want to wring her neck or throw a glass across the room, you're not ready to communicate yet.

You do not have to strike while the iron is hot. It is often best to wait till it cools off, when cooler heads prevail. Every emotion can be used in some way to create more movement, to open yourself to greater self-awareness and self-compassion. You can learn to use your anger for this outcome.

A goal for this chapter is to help you learn that your anger is your friend. As Julia Cameron wrote: "Anger is meant to be listened to. Anger is a voice, a shout, a plea, a demand. Anger is meant to be respected. Why? Because anger is a map. Anger shows us what our boundaries are." If you are afraid of feeling angry, then you're probably afraid of expressing your needs. If you are willing to befriend your angry feelings and communicate in a productive way, then change can happen.

When you give in to the urge to lash out, you may feel some relief in that initial moment, but then there is a whole lot of debris to clean up. When you lash out at somebody verbally or physically, what damage is caused in that initial explosion, in that initial reaction? Now the conversation will be about the action that was taken—the explosion—in whatever form it took (verbal or physical), instead of the problem that triggered the outburst. Those are very different issues and feelings to wrestle with and a whole different conversation. Anger really does not have to cause harm to you or anyone else.

Another goal is to learn to release your angry energy in a safe way. We deal with this a lot in the support group, because everyone benefits from new ideas and strategies in handling angry feelings. It isn't just for those who have anger management issues. Think about the fact that Carla didn't have anger management issues in general in her life, but the anger that erupted in her conversations with her mother had become debilitating for her. As she listened to the group, Carla began taking better care of herself, set healthier boundaries, and stopped reacting to her mother's criticisms and hostility. Carla felt calmer and was able to handle her mother's outbursts with greater compassion and understanding, rather than equal hostility. Her mother didn't change, but Carla's responses to her mother did, so their relationship seemed less stressful to Carla.

Here are five steps for processing through your angry feelings so you can actually move forward:

1. **And we breathe.** This is the first step in moving from reacting to being able to respond more thoughtfully and productively.

2. **Do a brain dump.** Without censoring, write down your thoughts and your feelings about the situation that has triggered your anger. Take twenty minutes or three pages, whichever comes first. Usually, you will come to an awareness, an aha moment that helps you get to the next step.

3. **Walk away and take a time-out.** This allows you time to clear your head, gather your thoughts, and determine how you want to handle the situation.

4. **What is your desired outcome?** Think about what you really want or need that came up in this situation. What became evident for you from your brain dump and time-out?

5. **Talk it out.** Discuss it with either with a friend or trusted advisor, especially if you still need to vent. This will help to ensure you have clarity as to what you need to say to resolve or more effectively manage the situation that triggered your strong reaction. Remember, "Anger is meant to be acted upon. It is not meant to be acted out."

When you're ready, communicate with the other person involved, stick to the specific issue(s), and start by stating your desired outcome. Be clear, direct, and focused and remember to breathe. Knowing your desired outcome is absolutely crucial; it's not about the story or the drama. It's not about blaming or finding fault; it's about expressing your feelings and goals in order to move forward in a positive direction for yourself.

And we breathe…

Chapter 5 Worksheet

Anger and Resentment:
The Obstacles and the Gifts

1. What do I do with my angry or resentful feelings?

   a. Implode (become depressed, hypertensive, and so on):

   _____

   b. Explode (rage against others or situations):

   _____

   c. Become passive-aggressive (silently get back at someone, become a martyr, and so on):

   _____

2. In what ways do these behaviors enhance, empower, undermine, or sabotage my self-care? No judgments, just awareness:

   _____

   _____

   _____

3. What are other options for dealing effectively with my anger and resentment?

   _____

   _____

   _____

4. Dealing with Anger is an A.R.T.

   a. Acceptance: How can I accept what I feel?

    _____

    _____

   b. Respect: Am I able to respect and not judge what I feel?

    _____

    _____

   c. Time: Am I willing to give myself time to process and work through what I feel?

    _____

    _____

Anger, resentment and jealousy don't change the
heart of others. They only change yours.

—*Shannon Alder,* 300 Questions to Ask Your
Parents Before It's Too Late

More Tools for Change: Sample Dialogue for a Big Change

IN SAM'S STORY, HE EXPRESSED concern about his parents' driving, a common concern for many caregivers of elderly parents. Asking our parents to give up driving is one of the more difficult conversations to have. It is, however, one of the most important, because it isn't just about them. Driving, as we all know, has an impact on many people and potentially on many lives, so it is a very necessary conversation. There are a few ways to address this very serious issue:

1. You can be a passenger with your parent to assess how he's driving. This gives you firsthand knowledge of her driving and you can address the problems right away.
2. You can discuss her driving with her primary care physician (or ophthalmologist, or neurologist, and so on) when you attend an appointment with her. Doctors will often be willing to address this issue.
3. You can ask your mother how she feels driving. Is she aware that her abilities have changed?
4. If you have siblings, make sure all of you are on the same page so everyone is supportive of this change in your father's life.

When you have the conversation:

1. **Acknowledge that this is a big issue for your parent.** Driving gives one an enormous sense of independence and, as physical abilities begin to wane, people want to hang on to whatever vestiges of independence they still have. Driving also makes one feel less isolated, so it's imperative that you respect how significant this change is.
2. **Be compassionate but firm.** Allow your parent to express her feelings, however vociferous they may be. Do not take it personally. This will be a huge adjustment for them initially, but it is for her (and others') greater good.

3. **Give your parents time to adjust to new ideas for transportation.** Don't rush in to minimize the adjustment period, but let them know that there are options for getting around.

4. **Be aware of options for transportation for your parent:**
   a. Personal driver they can call as needed or an aide who can drive them wherever they need or want to go.
   b. Senior transportation services in their local area.
   c. Uber or Lyft car service.
   d. Contract with a local, reputable taxi company.
   e. You or your siblings who might be available at different times.

This is an important issue and one that should not be taken lightly. Please reach out if this feels too overwhelming, or if you get a lot of resistance.

Chapter 6
Overcoming Guilt, Shame,
and Emotional Blackmail

*Emotional blackmail is the use of fear, obligation
and guilt to control another person.*

—*Susan Forward, PhD,* Emotional Blackmail

LET'S START WITH A CLEAR and direct understanding of each issue, starting with guilt. Guilt is a helpful emotion when it is justified. It motivates us to learn from our mistakes and make a change when warranted.

When you do something wrong, it's appropriate to feel guilty. It means you have a conscience, and you'll want to do something to make up for your mistake. Maybe a simple apology is enough, or maybe making amends is appropriate.

Shame is a sense of worthlessness or inadequacy about aspects of yourself or in your basic nature. Shame is frequently an offshoot of guilty feelings. Shame is fear-based and drives you to want to hide or protect yourself from scrutiny. It is hardly ever a helpful or motivating emotion.

The difference between guilt and shame is, guilt is feeling bad about what you do; shame is feeling bad about who you are.

Emotional blackmail occurs when others threaten you with abandonment, withholding their love, or punishment if you don't do things the right way (translate to, "their way"). You may also be using emotional blackmail to get your needs met, because that is how you learned to communicate. You might use emotional blackmail when you feel like a victim and use feeling powerless or weak as a means of getting what you want.

Guilt, when inappropriate or unjustified, is not only self-generated. It is often induced by others, and that is emotional blackmail. If you give in to these tactics, you feel bad about yourself, perhaps angry and resentful as well. If you stand up to them and feel others' disappointment, anger, pain, and the like, you then believe that you're wrong or bad and go down the road of guilt-induced shame.

In many situations you'll have feelings that will be difficult, uncomfortable, painful, or disturbing, regardless of the decision you make. *You* have to choose between dealing with the feelings generated when you disappoint someone else, or disappoint yourself. This may be the most difficult question to ask and answer, because it really is at the heart of guilt and shame: Are you willing and able to live with your integrity and self-respect even if it means someone else may feel betrayed, hurt, disappointed, and/or angry?

> *I want to know if you can disappoint another to be*
> *true to yourself; if you can bear the accusation of*
> *betrayal and not betray your own soul.*

—*Oriah Mountain Dreamer*, The Invitation

This book is all about learning to take as good care of yourself as you do of others in your life; healing from guilt and shame and ending the cycle of emotional blackmail is an enormously important part of self-care. When you respond to guilt-induced messages, it is imperative that you ask yourself who it is you are caring for and at what cost.

Symptoms of Self-Induced Guilt and Shame:

1. Feeling an overwhelming sense of responsibility for others' behaviors.
2. Feeling an ongoing sense of regret for your past behaviors (real or perceived).
3. Feeling burdened by your thoughts, feelings, or attitudes that are judgmental, critical, or negative of yourself or others.
4. Feeling pressured to please, help, or placate others at your own emotional expense.
5. Feeling stress or anxiety or both at setting a boundary with others.
6. Feeling a need to fix, manage, or take care of others' problems, difficulties, or circumstances so that they don't have to feel bad.
7. Taking care of and respecting your needs, and then feeling as if you did something wrong.
8. Feeling as if you have no choices and can only behave the way others expect you to behave.
9. Feeling an intense need or desire to amend your past.
10. Often lashing out at or blaming others for problems to mask your feelings of inadequacy.

The following are some messages from others that induce guilt and shame within you. They also are representative of signs of emotional blackmail.

1. You're told you're wrong in your actions or feelings and you accept this as true.
2. You accept blame for someone else's suffering.
3. You believe it when someone tells you that there is only one right way to do things.
4. You're convinced to go against your own needs, values, or beliefs to please someone else.
5. You're threatened with negative consequences, as in, "I'll fall apart and die if you don't do this for me," "You'll be eternally damned if you_____," "I'll never speak to you again," "No one will like you if you_____," and you then feel obligated to behave the way the other person wants, needs, or expects.
6. You frequently feel guilt-ridden, overwhelmed, and inadequate in all you do, not just in how you care for your loved ones.

If you can relate to any of these messages, then you know that you feel guilt and shame, and therefore you are more likely to be the victim of emotional blackmail. It takes a lot of practice, patience, and perseverance to eliminate guilt and shame from our lives, especially since it's rooted in many religions and cultures, and not just in our interpersonal relationships or within our own psyches. Remember, however, it can be done.

The topic of guilt, shame, and emotional blackmail is a book in its own right, but for our purposes, it is a step that needs to be addressed in order to move forward to take as good care of yourself as you do of others in your life. We deal with this issue extensively in the Take Back Your Life group program, as many caregivers feel burdened with guilt and subjected to emotional blackmail, either by those they're caring for or by other family members. Here are five basic steps to start practicing in order to move in a new direction while dealing with the responsibilities and stress of caregiving. You deserve to provide loving care to yourself and others without the burdens of guilt and shame.

Steps to Overcome and Eliminate Guilt from Your Life:

1. **And we breathe.** This first step is critical, because it gets you to be conscious and aware of your feelings, your behaviors, and the messages that you're reacting to. Before you can make changes in your attitudes and behaviors, you have to first be aware of them. This step gives you the time in which to do that.

2. **What's your desired outcome?** Be clear and direct, for yourself. You may want to live guilt-free, or have feelings of peace, serenity, joy, happiness, and ease. These goals, themselves, can initially produce guilty feelings. Your choice will be to either continue to behave in ways that undermine your power and self-esteem or to make new decisions that honor your integrity and positive feelings of self-worth. Ask yourself what you're willing to do to achieve your desired outcome. (Go back to your Step-by-Step guide for specific

situations. Download at www.lorenGelbergGoff.com/sbsg-tbyl or see Appendix 1.)

3. **Define the problem.** Write it out, analyze it clearly—just the facts, no emotion. Become aware of whose problem this really is. The guilt may be yours, but the problem may be someone else's and it's something they have to deal with, not you. Perhaps you can delegate this task to someone else—remember about asking for help?

4. **Do you want to feel the discomfort of disappointing yourself, or someone else?** Your integrity is at stake when guilt and shame appear in your life. This step helps you acknowledge whether you're willing to stand up for your own needs and integrity. There is no judgment here, simply awareness of what is really at stake. Every decision has consequences; you now get to decide which consequences you choose to accept. This step takes a lot of practice, so please remember to be patient with yourself.

5. **Place the oxygen mask on yourself first.** This step helps you make conscious and deliberate choices so that you can take better care of yourself physically, emotionally, and spiritually. With this step, you can consciously determine priorities for whose needs, feelings, or wishes you are taking care of and what you are realistically responsible for. This is not about *not* caring for someone else, it is about determining new ways of doing so that take *you* into consideration as well, because, yes, you do matter!

YES, CHANGING YOUR BEHAVIOR TAKES courage, and feelings of guilt will pop up when you simply consider making any of these changes. Take heart; this is normal. Guilt is a feeling, and it's not our feelings that get us into trouble, it's our actions. Your guilt will not dissipate if you continue giving in to the demands of your parents, and guilt will be around if you are not taking care of yourself, your spouse, or your children. Go back to Step 2 and ask yourself again: *What is my desired outcome?* Guilt implies that you are doing something wrong, but making changes does not mean you are doing something wrong; you are simply doing something differently. *And we breathe* through the urge to go back to an old, familiar pattern.

Just because someone demands something doesn't mean we have to respond. When parents say that they've lived too long, it absolutely can be their way of expressing their own frustration at their situation. Yes, it's hard to hear, and it's easy to jump in to console and deny their thoughts and feelings, but that is not necessary. You can acknowledge their frustration and angst without having to give in to their demands and attitude. This step also takes practice, patience, and perseverance.

Please note that while these steps are most necessary as you go forward in your life as a caregiver, they may not always be easy, and you may not always have the support you need, want, and deserve from the people in your life. Don't go it alone. There is help, support, and guidance, but you have to ask for it and be willing to receive it. Take that breath, focus on your needs and goals, and reach out!

I've been told many times over the years how lonely and isolating it is being a caregiver. It is part of what triggers beliefs that you have to go it alone, be a martyr, be a superwoman or superman which, of course, leads to fatigue and burnout. Guilt gets triggered when you believe that there's something wrong with you because you either don't want to, or cannot, do everything and handle everything. Go through the five steps each and every time these guilty feelings pop up and see how much they really can change. And remember, reach out. Help, guidance, and support are available.

And we breathe...

Chapter 6 Worksheet
Overcoming Guilt, Shame, and Emotional Blackmail

Guilt is:

_____

Shame is:

_____

The difference between guilt and shame is:

_____

_____

1. Guilt or shame show up in my life as a caregiver in these ways:

   _____

   _____

   _____

2. What guilt am I carrying?

   _____

   _____

   _____

3. What is the learning opportunity my guilt presents?

   _____

   _____

   _____

4. In my life, I have learned and absorbed shame-based beliefs. The following messages became my beliefs and they cause me to feel shame:

_____

_____

_____

5. Am I willing to challenge these beliefs, and what would I be willing to do differently as a result? List new attitudes, behaviors, and goals here:

_____

_____

_____

More Tools for Change:
Dialogue for Feelings of Guilt or Shame

*Never underestimate the courage you have or your
ability to do things you never did before.*

—*Hermann J. Steinherr,* international professor
and business coach

Here's a sample dialogue that can be helpful when your feelings of guilt or shame arise:

Mom: You haven't visited in a while and I miss you. You know there's not much an old lady like me can do on her own, so when you're not here I'm pretty much stuck.

You: (deep breath) I understand, Mom. I realize that your activities are limited. (You may think that she doesn't take advantage of senior programs and transportation options and chooses to only rely on you, but you leave it with this one statement.)

Mom: I know you're busy, but I really think I deserve some of your time and I'm sure you can make time if you really tried. I guess I'm just not a priority for you anymore.

You: (slow deep breath) Thank you, Mom, for recognizing that I am busy. I appreciate your concern for me (not going down the road of defending, explaining, or justifying). What is it you would like to do when I visit?

Mom: I don't know. We don't have to do much; it would just be nice to visit. Maybe we could go to lunch. I haven't been to a restaurant in a long time. You made me give up my license and my car, so I can't go anywhere now, can I? I have to wait for you to come and visit.

You: I'd love to take you to lunch. Where would you like to go? I can come next Sunday. Let's make that a date for us. I'll look forward to our visit. (Do not get caught in defending or justifying the statement about giving up driving.)

Mom: Well, if that's the best you can do, I guess I don't have a choice in the matter (deep sigh of resignation). I don't know what you want me to say. I guess I'll just have to wait until then for a visit.

YOU: (In spite of the twist in your gut, or pain in your chest, you breathe slowly and deeply.) That's great, Mom. We're on for next Sunday. In the meantime, did you want to go to the senior center tomorrow? I can arrange to have the van pick you up.

MOM: No. I have no interest in hanging around with old people who have nothing in common with me. I'll simply have to wait until you manage to get here.

YOU: (deep breath as you refrain from any argument to convince her to change her mind to appease your guilt) Great, Mom. Then I'll see you next Sunday and talk with you tomorrow. Love you.

And we breathe…

Chapter 7
Forgiveness Is Key: Breaking Free from Anger, Resentment, and Guilt

*Anger makes you smaller, while forgiveness forces
you to grow beyond what you are.*

—*Cherie Carter-Scott, PhD,* If Life is a Game...
These Are the Rules

COMING FROM GUILT, SHAME, EMOTIONAL blackmail, and all
the hurt, anger, and frustration that go with them, we enter a new
realm of self-care: forgiveness.

Let's first define the word "forgiveness." The Merriam Webster
dictionary defines forgiveness as: "to pardon; to give up resentment
of; to cease to feel resentment against." I also define it as: letting
go; releasing oneself, emotionally, from a negative experience.

The words may sound relatively easy; it's the actions of giving
up, releasing, ceasing that cause people the most difficulty. As
caregivers, it's important to acknowledge your thoughts, feelings,
beliefs, and history about and with the person you are caring for.
It's also important to look at what your relationship has been and
is with other family members. Acknowledging the history that
has brought you to this point helps you understand what you are
carrying emotionally, so that you can decide how you want to
move forward in the care you are providing.

Forgiveness is a conscious decision and choice you make. Most of us were taught that when we felt hurt or slighted in some way, large or small, to let it go. Maybe even, if someone apologized, you were taught to say, "It's okay," "No problem," "Never mind," or some other phrase that would dismiss the event. However, these responses do not address the hurt or injury you sustained. In fact, when the response to an apology is "It's okay," you are essentially giving the offender permission to hurt you again. I am sure that is not your intention.

Many people grew up hearing the phrase "They didn't mean it." This implies that if someone says or does something hurtful, but it was unintentional or in a fit of anger, we're just supposed to ignore it and not address the real hurt that was inflicted. An appropriate or helpful response to someone when they apologize is, "Thank you for acknowledging what you did, and acknowledging my feelings in this matter." It is not necessary that you immediately say, "You are forgiven." Some offenses may require time to process, so it is appropriate to say, "Thank you and I'm working on forgiving."

Most people are not out to be mean, hurtful, and upsetting on purpose. Often people are unaware of the hurt they inflict by their actions and words. For some it's just what they are used to or what they've been allowed to do throughout their lives. Until they are called out and told that their behavior is unacceptable, they will continue to behave as they always have.

Sandy's Story

SANDY, A WOMAN IN OUR Take Back Your Life group program, was caring for her parents, who were becoming frailer and in need of increasing help and assistance each day. She shared these responsibilities with her sisters, who were also very involved. It always appeared that things were going well, as her parents were well attended; however, there was a history of sibling rivalry, jealousy, and hurt that had never been resolved. Sandy had always felt rejected by her sisters and had received the message throughout her life that she just didn't measure up.

Somehow, her sisters always got more credit and attention and they, in their own ways, lorded it over Sandy. Comments would be made that sounded and seemed like put-downs, and throughout Sandy's lifetime of enduring these attitudes and behaviors, her mother would always say, "Let it go; they don't mean it." So, ignoring her feelings became Sandy's primary coping skill whenever she felt hurt, insulted, demeaned, or ignored, especially by family members.

It was evident that in order for Sandy to continue to participate in her parents' care and maintain some semblance of a relationship with her siblings, she had to decide how she wanted to take care of herself in the face of the history of injuries she had been carrying and the real impact they had and were having on her self-esteem and self-confidence, and on relationships in her life—not just the relationships with her sisters. We create patterns based upon our beliefs about others as well as ourselves, and those beliefs dictate our behaviors. And, of course, our behaviors determine outcomes.

It was hard for Sandy to talk about her own struggles when dealing with her parents' needs, because she always felt she was being judged and criticized. If someone asked a question about her parents' needs and the care provided, she would become defensive and withdraw from the conversation, or say, "You just don't understand." We all have stock answers when we feel defensive because we come from a space of feeling criticized and judged. Remember the statement: "Don't believe everything you think." Just because something may have been true in the past or seems true today doesn't mean it really is true.

Remember the definition of insanity? Doing the same thing over and over again and expecting different results. Sandy had to decide on some new behaviors, but first she had to understand and learn about forgiveness. Sandy always hoped that somehow, someway, if she didn't let them know how much they hurt her or how angry she had been over the years, that they would change and undo what had occurred. She thought that surely they would realize how hurtful their behavior was and see the damage it was causing. Unfortunately, without any direct communication, nothing can change. The person with whom you have to communicate your feelings, first and foremost, is you, yourself. The challenge of feeling vulnerable is a big one, but a necessary one as you move forward.

What behavior will you no longer accept or tolerate? Are you ready to set new, clear, healthy boundaries? While we cannot change what happened in the past, we can change how we view it, and what we can learn from it. Forgiveness is *not* about rewriting history; it is about viewing it from a new perspective and with new awareness and insights.

> *Forgiveness is letting go of all hope for a better past.*
>
> —*Anonymous*

Here are some steps we worked on in our group to understand and work through the feelings of any event or circumstance:

1. **I acknowledge who you are and that I have no control or power to make you be someone different.** Who is the person you're thinking of? Without judgments, list the qualities this person has. Is he or she sensitive, shy, hostile, controlling, insensitive, or the like? Just list the qualities and acknowledge that this is who she or he is and you do not have the power to change him or her. Take a deep breath and note how difficult or easy this step is for you. Do you hear any "yes, buts" in your mind (for example, "Yes, I know he's arrogant, but he shouldn't be")? Take a deep breath and allow yourself to sit with who this person is and how you feel about them. Is this someone you respect, love, admire, need, resent? Pay attention to your thoughts and feelings without judging them. This step frees you from the unrealistic belief or expectation that you can change the other person.

2. **I acknowledge my part in this event.** Even if you were a victim, acknowledge your role. Acknowledge what your thoughts and feelings were or are in regard to having been powerless in this event, for not knowing better, for your lack of awareness, for your wish to have handled the situation differently. Write down whatever you remember your part was.

3. **I acknowledge whatever pain and suffering I have endured as a result of this event.** Write down what feelings, beliefs, and thoughts you have carried within you about this person or event since it occurred. When you feel the judgments creep back in, *Stop! Breathe! Focus!* Allow yourself to be aware of where you carry these feeling in your body and how strong they are. What do they tell you? How

do these feelings keep you stuck in the past and reactive in the present whenever this circumstance or person are remembered or mentioned?

4. **From this event, I learn something valuable for myself and my life going forward.** What can you learn about yourself, other people, circumstances, that will enhance your life? Every event is a learning experience *if we allow it*. The Danish philosopher Soren Kierkegaard is quoted as saying, "Life can only be understood backwards; but it must be lived forwards." What do you now understand about that person or event that will help you going forward in your life? I don't mean you should say, "I'll never do that again," but rather see the event as a life lesson. What did you learn about how you communicate, how you listen, how else you might handle a situation like that in the future? Once you get past the judgments of yourself and others and you are sitting with just your awareness, learning can take place.

5. **What is my desired outcome?** Do you want to feel more empowered and be open to new possibilities for yourself? Allow yourself to learn a life lesson, and in this step you can create that goal.

Sandy had to work hard to let go of the beliefs and judgments she had long held about her sisters, so that she could move forward in her desired outcome to provide the care and support she wanted to give to her parents as they aged. Sandy came to the awareness that her sisters had insecurities, fears, and doubts about themselves and their lives, but communicated and handled them differently than she did. She was able to respect the pain that she had endured through her life as a result of their hurtful comments and knew that she could never convince them that they were wrong, bad, or mean to her. She knew that they saw themselves as loving people and she no longer had to react to them as if they were the enemy out to hurt her. She recognized that she had given in to all their demands in the past in the hope that then they'd love and respect her. She learned that this was not what had happened at all. By having been the one who constantly did their bidding, no matter how burdensome, she was simply reinforcing their negative, hurtful attitudes and behaviors.

This was an enormous life lesson because she came to realize that she was often mean and unloving toward her sisters because of her own hurt, resentment, and anger and that this made her seem wrong, bad, and mean to them. Sandy had to work through the steps to forgive herself, and she also learned that the grudges she was carrying toward her sisters had a negative impact on her behaviors toward them and even spilled over into other areas of her life. Many life lessons are challenging to embrace because they do feel painful. However, not addressing these lessons only keeps the feelings buried, continuing to wreak havoc on you internally and in your life. While the truth may set you free, no one ever said it would make you feel good. It's important to acknowledge and remember that *you have to feel it to heal it.*

Through the work Sandy did on forgiving her sisters, even though they were not at all involved in the process, Sandy made a huge change in her relationships with them as they shared in the responsibilities of caring for their parents. She was able to change how she communicated with them. She also created new boundaries that seemed more respectful of herself and her needs, always keeping in mind her desired outcome to provide loving care to their parents. Sandy and her sisters did not become best friends, but their ability to work together improved dramatically because Sandy was able to let go, release her pain and suffering, and forgive. Remember, forgiveness is *not* about anyone else, forgiveness is for you. *Forgiveness is a gift you give yourself.*

Forgiveness, as I stated before, is a decision you make. While many emotions are released through the work of forgiveness, the initial step is a choice, a conscious decision that you make. Many books are written about forgiveness, as it is an important part of life's journey. In this book, I want to focus on the importance of forgiving so that you really can take as good care of yourself as you do of others in your life.

Forgiveness is the feeling of peace that emerges as you take your hurt less personally, take responsibility for how you feel, and become a hero instead of a victim in the story you tell. Forgiveness is the experience of peacefulness in the present moment. Forgiveness does not change the past, but it changes the present. Forgiveness means that even though you are wounded, you choose to hurt and suffer less. Forgiveness means you become a part of a solution. Forgiveness is the understanding that hurt is a normal part of life. Forgiveness is for you and no one else. You can forgive and rejoin a relationship or forgive and never speak to the person again.

—*Fred Luskin,* Forgive for Good

Life is forever presenting us with people, situations, events, and circumstances that we will judge as either good or bad, depending on the feelings and perceptions that they evoke within us. If, however, you are able to see every event, circumstance, or situation as a learning opportunity, then handling the situation in a new and less reactive way is more likely. Our life lessons usually come as a result of our greatest challenges. These learning opportunities can be seen as gifts in black wrapping. No, they hardly look like gifts, but when you are able to learn, grow, and evolve from these moments, they are gifts, and we can then forgive these moments by taking the judgments of them out of our daily life. When you are caring for your aging parents, alone or with family, your history is part of the story, and your history provides many lessons, opportunities for growth, and ongoing relationships that provide gifts in black wrapping.

Sarah's Story

WHEN SARAH'S HUSBAND WAS DIAGNOSED with the same cancer her father had, which she had believed resulted from his refusal to ever go to a doctor, Sarah's husband's illness became a big gift in black wrapping for her. She needed to work on forgiveness toward her father, whose debilitating illness still caused her extreme upset in her adult life, and she had to work through her feelings of fear, anger, and resentment that she felt toward her husband so that they could deal with the consequences and changes that this diagnosis brought into their lives.

Sarah had to decide that she could, in fact, connect to learning about forgiveness because she wanted to be able to be there for her husband in a loving and respectful way. This was her desired outcome. She went through the four steps previously described, and there were days when she went through them again. Do not expect that forgiveness of a situation or person is done once and it never needs to be looked at again. Forgiveness is a process. As the writer and professor Mason Cooley stated, "Forgiveness is like faith. You have to keep reviving it."

So, do not be disheartened when old feelings reemerge, or situations and behaviors of others continue to pop up. These are the curves life throws; I always refer to them as "pop quizzes." Remember how, in school, the teacher would announce as you walked through the door: "Okay, books away, pens out, we're having a pop quiz." Remember how you felt—anxious, scared, worried, stressed? Did you do the required reading? Did you remember what was reviewed in class? Doubts, questions, and fears would race through you. Well, in school, you got a lesson and then the quiz. In life we get the pop quiz and then the lesson. These pop quizzes are often gifts in black wrapping, if we allow it.

Oftentimes, the pop quiz shows up to test your resolve. Are you committed to your goal, to your desired outcome? Are you remembering that forgiveness is for you and that it's not about the other person? It's easy to be thrown off track when old situations show up or people behave in the same old ways. That is when you can review the steps outlined in this chapter and do the workbook pages that follow this chapter to further learn, grow, and evolve in the work of forgiveness.

Before you work on relationships, issues, and challenges that require you to find forgiveness so that you can heal, let's review a few specifics about what forgiveness is and what it is not.

Forgiveness Is Not:

1. **Forgetting.** We don't forget the offense, we learn and grow from it.
2. **Restoring the same relationship.** A relationship may be closer than before, or not; sometimes forgiving means you can leave the relationship behind.
3. **Removal of consequences.** It is not about saying what was done was okay. There can still be consequences.
4. **Ignoring the offense.** You don't pretend nothing happened when you forgive. An offense occurred. Pretending as if it never happened only builds resentment and anger.
5. **An immediate emotional healing.** Emotions heal with time. Some pains run deeper and take longer to heal.
6. **Rewriting history.** You are not pretending the event never occurred; you are shifting your perspective so that your history no longer controls or detracts from your present.
7. **Revenge.** It's not about getting back at anyone or making anyone else suffer because of an injury done to you.

Forgiveness Is:

1. **For you, not anyone else.** It doesn't matter if anyone apologizes, letting go is a gift you give yourself for freedom, relief, and less drama in your life.
2. **Letting go of expectations of others or situations that are out of your control.** Forgiveness means recognizing that there are many "unenforceable rules," as Fred Luskin terms them, which you need to learn to accept; remind

yourself that acceptance doesn't mean liking someone or something.

3. **Letting go of the victim role.** You are not a victim, even if you were in the past, and you can now choose how you handle past events and the lessons they bring to you today for your growth and overall well-being.

4. **Letting go of judgments of right vs. wrong.** You are willing to see each event as a learning opportunity.

5. **Letting go of unenforceable rules.** Unenforceable rules are how you think others *should* behave or what a situation *should* have been. It's important to be aware of the rules you live by, and that you cannot obligate others to do the same. (Remember that a desired outcome has to be something over which you have control.)

6. **Willingness to take responsibility for your part.** Whatever your part may have been, this connects you to your humanity and feelings of compassion for yourself and others.

7. **Letting go of all hope for a better past.** Wishing the past event didn't occur will not undo it. You are able to work through your feelings with understanding and compassion to promote learning, growth, and change.

These truths hold whether you are forgiving someone else or yourself. We are usually our own worst critics, as we tend to be harder on ourselves than on anyone else. We also tend to struggle more with self-forgiveness than with forgiving others. When you forgive yourself, it means you are willing to let go of self-criticism, self-deprecation, and self-loathing. It means you are willing to see yourself through loving eyes, even if everything you have said, thought, or done did not always feel loving. Part of the process in forgiving is a willingness to see what your loving intentions are or were when events didn't quite turn out the way you planned.

For example, Alice placed her mother in an assisted living facility about a year before her death. This decision was made because Alice worked full-time, her mother needed more care than they could provide at home, and Alice was plain exhausted. Her mother had always said she wanted to stay at home or live with her daughter and never wanted to be placed anywhere. This wish could not, ultimately, be granted.

As her mother's needs increased, Alice became increasingly angry and frustrated, and their relationship no longer felt loving and compassionate. Upon making the decision to have her mother live in assisted living, a myriad feelings came up, including a great deal of guilt, shame, and anger as well as relief. Many arguments ensued, and throughout the year we did a lot of work on forgiveness. The first step in this process was connecting to loving intentions. There was a desired outcome for her mother to feel loved, be safe, and have good quality life. None of these outcomes was being achieved while her mother lived at home. Even though moving into assisted living was not what was originally desired or planned, it turned out to be the best decision overall. There were many feelings of hurt and disappointment, as well as feelings of inadequacy that needed to be worked through.

It's important to understand that forgiveness doesn't mean everything is perfect. It means that you let go of the pain, anger, resentment, and fear that you have felt and that there is no wish for your own or anyone else's suffering.

> Forgiveness is not always easy. At times, it feels more painful than the wound we suffered, to forgive the one that inflicted it. And yet, there is no peace without forgiveness. Attack thoughts towards others are attack thoughts towards ourselves. The first step in forgiveness is the willingness to forgive.
> —Marianne Williamson, *A Course in Miracles*

Everyone tells me that they have reasons not to forgive, but the reality is that, without forgiveness, you cannot really move forward with your desired outcome for providing loving care to those in your life. Life will always present you with hurts, disappointments, frustrations, and upsets. As long you hold on to these injuries, the person or event who caused them owns you. They live in your mind and heart rent-free, and they are very destructive tenants.

Whatever reasons you may have not to forgive, or say forgiving doesn't really matter, the reality is that by holding onto hurt, shame, anger, resentment, or guilt you create an environment within yourself that is ripe for depression, an inability to fully give love or receive love, and a tendency toward more addictive behaviors (around food, drugs, work, busyness, and so on). Not forgiving keeps you stuck, and you remain a victim of the event or person. Not forgiving has a strong physical impact as well. The Johns Hopkins medicine website, and its article, "Forgiveness: Your Health Depends on It," is one of many sources that tells us that not forgiving can lead to digestive problems, headaches, fatigue, heart problems and inflammatory diseases, to name just a few physical ailments.

As I stated earlier, there are tomes written on forgiveness. My goal here is to help you open up to the idea and importance of forgiveness so that you really can take as good care of yourself as you do of the others in your life.

Please go on to the workbook pages and choose an event or person in your life that is a destructive tenant taking up space in your head or heart and that you'd like to release. You can always reach out to me for added support, guidance, and encouragement in how to embrace forgiveness in your life. http://lorengelberggoff. com/contact/

And we breathe...

Chapter 7 Worksheet

Forgiveness Is Key: Breaking Free from Anger, Resentment, and Guilt

1. I choose to shift my perspective on a situation: (Use additional pages as needed.)

   a. I write my story here about my anger, resentment and/or guilt. (Include all the hurt, anger, resentment, guilt, and so on. Hold nothing back.)

   _____

   _____

   _____

   _____

   b. I write my story a second time including any new awareness, insights, or perspectives on the situation that I now see.

   _____

   _____

   _____

   _____

   c. I write my story a third time, including what I've learned and how I might see the situation differently than I did initially. This includes reframing the situation to one that includes acknowledgment of learning and growth and compassion for myself as well as for the other person or situation.

   _____

_____

_____

_____

2. Am I ready to see this event, situation, or relationship as a way for me to heal my past so that I learn and grow for my present and future? (Remember the gift in black wrapping.) Or what still gets in my way as I strive to achieve my desired outcome for peace, happiness, serenity within?

_____

_____

_____

_____

_____

_____

_____

*In forgiving, I am learning to honor the love,
not the pain.*

—*David Kessler*

More Tools for Change: Mantra for Forgiveness

HO'OPONOPONO IS AN ANCESTRAL HAWAIIAN practice in which people get in touch with their anger, accept their errors (both are accepted causes of disease for this culture), and work on them until their burden disappears.

This is the meditation:

I am responsible for_____ (whatever my role was in this situation).

I'm sorry. (take a slow deep breath)

Forgive me. (take a slow deep breath)

I love you. (take a slow deep breath)

Thank you. (take a slow deep breath)

Repeat 3 times or more as needed for any given situation.

Chapter 8
Making Changes:
What Do I Really Fear?

Getting over a painful experience is much like crossing monkey bars. You have to let go at some point in order to move forward.

—C.S. Lewis

MAKING CHANGES IN YOUR ATTITUDE and behavior as you care for those you love takes courage. Implementing changes also requires practice, patience, and perseverance. Just as you read about the process of forgiveness—taking time and needing to revisit some issues repeatedly—change is also more than a one-shot cure.

To change, you must begin somewhere. It starts with awareness. You feel unhappy, frustrated, upset, or angry about some aspect of your life. As a caregiver, the feelings may revolve around the enormous responsibilities, obligations, stresses, and tensions that you face every day. They may revolve around setting new boundaries, being able to say no to some of the ongoing daily requests and demands. Maybe the changes you need to make involve your relationships with other family members. Whatever the issues, change brings up many stressors that too many people try very hard to avoid. The reality is, whether or not you make a change in your attitude or behavior, you will feel stress. It's simply a matter of which stress you will deal with: the stress of the same old, same old or the stress of doing something new and different.

As you go through this book and work through the different ways of seeing your responsibilities, your relationships, and your life, your awareness of your needs and feelings will increase. As your awareness grows, so, too, does your desire for something different. Change is inevitable, whether it happens actively or passively. You are dealing with someone who is in need of care; their health is compromised. Whether it is age-related, a chronic illness, or another kind of debilitating illness, changes are going to happen, and this chapter is about the ability to make changes that will best take care of you as you continue to love and care for those in your life.

We are living in fast-paced times, with very little space for stopping, breathing, and reflecting. Many people struggle with taking it slow because of fear of missing out (FOMO). There seems to be a clear judgment that if someone is not super busy (meaning working a full-time job as well as engaging in leisure activities), then they have plenty of time to devote to caregiving. This perception adds to your already incredibly busy and stressful life in ways that are sometimes hard to discern.

As caregivers, you often operate on autopilot, which means you haven't necessarily even thought about changing anything. You're too busy making sure you put one foot in front of the other so that you can get through your day. Yet, with feelings of dissatisfaction, frustration, stress, anxiety, or simply resignation that "it is what it is," making a change or changes seems out of the realm of possibility. Are you feeling the sadness that creeps in with this statement? Are you feeling the stress of somehow explaining, defending, and justifying all you do and why time is so limited? Are you feeling the frustration that comes with trying to convince others in your family to understand how exhausted and spent you feel?

Changes are possible! As I've stated before, you have to start with awareness. We don't or can't change anything without an awareness that we want something to be different.

Often the desire for change begins with vague feelings of frustration or wishes for something else in your life. At this point many people will tell me that they have to wait for the right moment or for someone to give them permission to do something differently. Here's the reality of life. Author and publisher William Feather said it spot on: "Conditions are never just right. People who delay action until all factors are favorable are the kind who do nothing." This is very true for caregivers.

Fear of change comes in many guises. We may not want to upset the precarious balance that we have established thus far. We may be fearful of others' reactions to our changes in behavior, demeanor, or attitude. Fear may show up as doubt or uncertainty as to whether or not changes we make will really improve our lives, along the lines of *I'm used to and familiar with what's going on,* or *I don't know if I can handle the upheaval I fear change will bring.*

Lorraine's Story

THINK ABOUT WHAT HOLDS YOU BACK from making and asserting changes in your activities, routine, and life. One woman, Lorraine, told me that making the change in how much she took care of for her mother—by limiting her visits or delegating some responsibilities to other family members or even her mother's friends—meant people in her life (translate to siblings) would be angry and critical of her decisions. She told me that it would be too hard to listen to their criticisms and judgments of her if she changed or gave up some of what she handled for their mother. She had been told many times that because she didn't work outside the home, "What else did she have to do? Of course she could devote her days and often evenings and nights to providing care and assistance for their mother." This was her life for about three years before we met and she was able to start to make some strategic changes in her life.

Lorraine had always been a caregiver. She had felt responsible for her mother through her tumultuous years growing up, cared for her mother through years of depression after her parents split up, and cared for her later in life, too, when her mother was riddled with both medical and physical ailments that further limited her independence. Lorraine was the one the family turned to for answers.

Now, as Lorraine became a senior citizen with her own adult children and grandchildren, she felt trapped and believed that she had no one to turn to for support or help. She was so used to doing everything on her own and never asking for help that her siblings had simply grown used to this reality and seemed to never even think about how Lorraine might feel or that she might want or need any help from them.

To begin the work of making changes in this scenario, Lorraine had to first be willing to acknowledge that she was aware that she was uncomfortable, even unhappy at times, with how things were going in her life. She also had to admit that to make any change, she'd have to give up some control over her mother's life and decisions that she had grown used to making.

We started with her biggest challenge. What was it that caused her the most stress in her role as caregiver? Lorraine's biggest stress was never having a weekend off to spend with her husband and grandchildren. She was always on call for her mother, so a weekend away never happened. This was a source of great sadness and frustration. Because no one ever offered to take Mom for a weekend, Lorraine didn't believe that she could ask.

It's not that Lorraine didn't think of wanting to ask her siblings for help, it was simply that she believed, because they never had stepped up to offer, that they just wouldn't help. She had been the sole caregiver for so long that it was simply automatic for her to take everything on without reaching out for help. When her husband asked her to take time off, she would tell him it wasn't possible. While this was a major source of stress in their marriage, they powered on. He would occasionally go visit their children and grandchildren for weekends when they couldn't come to their grandparents, and this gave him a break, but added to the guilt and frustration both he and Lorraine felt.

Lorraine and I began working together in earnest to create a change. Her first priority was to have a weekend off. I shared the Caregiver's Step-by-Step Guide so that she could clearly see the steps necessary to effect this change in her life. It's great to have a wish, a dream, or a fantasy, but our job was to make it a genuine desired outcome, and that meant putting a plan in place. We all need to see steps we can take to make a dream a reality.

Awareness is the first step. Lorraine was aware that she felt overwhelmed, sad, and trapped. She knew that she needed something to change, but continually had gotten stuck on how this would happen. The beliefs, habits, and patterns were so ingrained that nothing could change; she felt stymied at the starting block so she went no farther.

The desire for a change is often fraught with mixed feelings. Lorraine was eager for that weekend off, but was also fearful of a negative reaction or rejection from her siblings and even struggled with the idea of giving up control. As a caregiver, you often feel like you're in charge and that you can ensure that things are done your way. If someone else comes in for an hour, a day, a weekend, or longer, you have to give up that control. That is also an issue to work on because giving up control brings up many uncomfortable, stressful, and, for many people, anxious feelings. These are only some of the reasons why so many caregivers do not make changes.

You Are Enough

ANOTHER ISSUE THAT COMES UP for caregivers is that making a change will change their perceived status. Often caregivers get a lot of praise and appreciation for their devotion and hard work. While much of this recognition may fade, we hang on to the belief that it's still there. If you give up even a little bit of what you do in your role as a caregiver, it seems like a loss of status, value, and sense of self-worth. Making a change means we have to change this belief and perception. Live by this core message: **Who I Am Is Enough.**

You, as an individual, are enough; what you do for anyone else is the icing on the cake. Making a change will *not* undermine who you are and will *not* diminish your loving care for anyone. In fact, making changes that take good care of you will actually enhance your relationships with others because you will learn that you do not have to prove your worth. Who you are is enough!

Once you know what it is you want, work on the steps that help to make it a reality. Feelings always arise in the face of any change you may want to make. Fear, doubt, uncertainty, or maybe even disbelief are among the most common such feelings. Lorraine had to look at the options she had to create a weekend off. Options included asking siblings, hiring an aide for the weekend, asking neighbors and church members to look in on her mother at set times during the weekend and giving Lorraine a status update, and having her mother spend a weekend in a local assisted living facility using their respite care services.

Any of the above options was viable for Lorraine. She had to decide which one she would feel most able to explore. Yes, feelings always come up at this point, because it means you are taking your desire for change and taking a step into action. You have to make that call, investigate that option, face your fears, and take that step. You have to now realize that you must allow yourself the opportunity to feel better.

It's too easy to fall into the rut of stress. It actually requires no effort to feel stuck and overwhelmed. What requires effort is feeling good. In order to let go of stress, and feeling overwhelmed, you have to be willing to do something that is different than what you have been doing all along. You have to look at your beliefs that keep you stuck and ask yourself if you are allowed to feel good. I realize that sounds like a no-brainer, but many caregivers feel that it is normal, natural, and expected that they will feel this ongoing level of stress and upset. Many people have shared with me that they feel like something is missing when they feel relaxed, calm, and peaceful. This loss signifies to them that something is wrong. How often do you find yourself wondering the same thing?

Human beings are amazingly resilient, and we can handle so much and adapt to many situations, making even the most uncomfortable and stressful situations seem normal. As the saying goes, "normal is as normal does," and we can make most anything normal, including suffering. However, changing a habit, behavior, or belief means we have to change our definition of normal. It means we have to deal with the feelings that arise in the face of any change and not react to them, so that we can achieve a new definition of normal. When there is a crisis and everyone is running to the emergency room or hospital, running back and forth becomes normal very quickly, albeit stressful and upsetting. Everyone hopes it will be for a very short period of time. There is no time to think about what you need to do; you simply do it. When the situation becomes chronic, however, and schedules must be readjusted for the long-term, and you have to consciously think about your own needs, desired outcomes have to be looked at more clearly and directly. That means we need to address changes and create plans to adapt to a new normal.

Making changes doesn't mean you make life perfect. It means you accommodate, assess, and accept the reality of your circumstances and determine what changes are needed that will allow you to take as good care of yourself as you do of those you love. Acceptance of a situation doesn't mean you like it; it means you accept a reality. You may not like extreme weather conditions, but you accept them by dressing accordingly and making plans that take the weather conditions into consideration. That is a necessity of life. Caregiving is really no different. You may desperately want your parents to need less help, to be healthier, but they're not. Lorraine absolutely wanted her mother to be all right completely on her own so she could go away for a weekend as she used to do. This, however, was not the reality. Normal had changed over the course of a few years, and now Lorraine had to make changes that acknowledged the new normal.

THE DESIRE TO MAKE CHANGES has to be stronger than your fear of what others will say, think, or do. You do not have control over them or their reactions, so it is imperative that you breathe through your fears, doubts, uncertainties, and whatever else has contributed to your feeling stuck up until now. Breathing means you are giving yourself pause so that you can think clearly through a situation, a need, and a desired outcome, and not react out of habit or old beliefs.

Lorraine was able to decide that her desire to have a weekend off was worth exploring the options she came up with. She called her church and found that many members were willing to stop in throughout the weekend she was planning to be away. They would visit with her mother and see that she took her meds, which Lorraine set up, and they would call her or text her to give her updates. Lorraine and her husband went away for a weekend and discovered that she *could* do this again. She even worked up her courage to reach out to her siblings to get their help, so this would not have to be the one and only weekend off.

If you do not ask for something you need or want, the answer is always "no."

And we breathe…

Chapter 8 Worksheet

Making Changes: What Do I Really Fear?
What am I really afraid will happen if I change?

1. What is it I really want as I move forward in my role as a caregiver? What is my desired outcome?

   _____

   _____

2. What am I afraid will happen if I actually move in the direction of my desired outcome(s)?

   _____

   _____

3. Am I willing to breathe through my fears and create new behaviors and beliefs? List at least one new behavior I can practice that will open me up to feeling more positively about myself, my role and my life:

   _____

   _____

4. What feelings come up as I anticipate giving up the control I have in my role as caregiver and share responsibilities and burdens?

   _____

   _____

   _____

5. What empowerment do I experience by my decision to make
this change?

_____

_____

_____

*A year from now you will wish you
had started today.*

—*Karen Lamb, author*

More Tools for Change: A Daily Poem

"Through My Eyes"

If you could see yourself through my eyes,
You'd see how beautiful you are.
If you could see yourself through my eyes,
You'd see how you sparkle when you smile;
If you could see yourself through my eyes,
You'd see how you light up when you're just being you.
If you could see yourself through my eyes,
You would know that you shine from within.
If you could see yourself through my eyes,
You would know that who you are is a gift to anyone who
knows you.

—*Loren M. Gelberg-Goff*

It is helpful if you're willing to recite this poem while looking at a picture of yourself. Allow yourself these moments to connect to your worth, knowing deep down that you really are and always have been enough… *and we breathe.*

Chapter 9
Pop Quizzes: Oops, It Happened Again

Pop quizzes are events, circumstances, or interactions that bring up feelings and thoughts within you that reinforce and perpetuate past behaviors and beliefs that keep you stuck. They can be used as moments of growth and change or reasons to stay mired in old beliefs and habits.

ONE SPRING AFTERNOON, I WAS volunteering at my son's elementary school, and it was approaching the time I had to pick my daughter up from high school. There was about a twenty-minute difference between each school's final bell. I was stressing, leaving my son's school to race to my daughter's school and desperately trying to figure out how I was going to manage to pick them both up on time. I raced out of my son's school to get to my car, so that I could be on time when my daughter got out of school.

Halfway to my daughter's school, while stopped at a light, I managed to take a deep breath. I thought about the insanity of my behavior. I realized that I needed to rethink. I felt stressed, overwhelmed, and burdened as I saw myself in the loop of doing everything perfectly. I continued driving to my daughter's school, aggravated with myself that I hadn't stopped to think before I raced out of my son's school on a schedule to which I had ceded my power.

Later that afternoon, having retrieved both my children from their respective schools, relatively on time, I was able to come up with other options for this particular situation. This was the when the birth of the Caregiver's Step-by-Step guide began. It struck me how often we operate on autopilot and just do what we do without thinking, planning, or processing. It's no wonder we end up so frustrated, irritated, and exhausted.

I could have called a friend who would be at the high school to pick up her son and asked her to look for my daughter and drive her home. I could have sent a text to my daughter letting her know I'd be a few minutes late and to wait for me, or I could have told my son to wait and I'd be back for him. I also could have taken my son out of school twenty minutes early and then calmly driven to pick up my daughter.

Many things happen quickly, and we feel suddenly blindsided. Those are the moments when we most need to *Stop! Breathe! Focus!* and get our bearings. Even with years of practice, professionally and personally, I still get pop quizzes that remind me of the importance of self-care and more and more frequently I manage to shift gears before any action takes place. Those are the moments I celebrate.

I've talked about pop quizzes to help you handle issues of forgiveness, making changes, and setting boundaries. Here's a whole chapter devoted to handling life's pop quizzes.

As you make changes in your life that will enhance your journey to take as good care of yourself as you do of others in your life, pop quizzes will arise. Life continually throws us curves, and pop quizzes are the moments you face to check in with how important something is to you. Are you really committed to a new boundary, belief, attitude, or behavior? Are you trusting in your abilities to cope with the resistance you face from others and within yourself? Pop quizzes often show up in life to test your resolve. Pop quizzes are learning opportunities. It's important to consider a reality that in life, good experiences will produce memorable moments; bad experiences will produce lessons, or growth opportunities.

When you were in school, pop quizzes never felt good; they don't feel good in life either. However, they are going to occur, and you have choices as to how you want to handle these unexpected and usually upsetting and stressful moments. Practice taking that slow deep breath before responding to any situation. It will help you to become conscious and aware of the situation, your feelings, and clear a pathway to determine a desired outcome.

You are learning to respond to old issues and situations in new ways. A pop quiz helps you practice a new belief, attitude, or behavior so that you can become increasingly more comfortable with it. Maybe you've been talking about setting new boundaries with your mother, such as not dropping everything immediately to run an errand. Maybe you even shared this new plan with your spouse or best friend. You've said it enough times that you think it's doable, and your tension is manageable.

And then Mom calls to tell you she needs a few items from the grocery store, and how soon can you be there. Pop quiz! Feelings arise... and we breathe. This is the first time you will actually have to assert your new boundary, new desired outcome, and new attitude. Bernie Siegel, MD is an internationally recognized expert in the field of cancer treatment and complementary, holistic medicine and author who advises his patients to always focus on the positive power of making changes. His advice is, "Embrace each challenge in your life as an opportunity for self-transformation."

Strategies for Handling Life's Pop Quizzes

1. **And we breathe.** Take the ever-important slow, deep breath to give you pause. This step gives you a moment to collect your thoughts and feelings. Here's when you remind yourself that you are working on improving how you take care of yourself, that you do, in fact, matter.

2. **Ask, "What is my desired outcome?"** Remember this necessary question that must be asked and answered. It has to fulfill the following two requirements: It has to be what you want, not what you don't want, and it has to be something over which you have control.

3. **Acknowledge that you have heard the request.** You gain a little more breathing room if you repeat what you have heard. This lets the other person know that you have heard him and you understand what it is he wants or needs.

4. **Validate her need or feelings**. We all want to know that our needs and feelings matter and we love when someone gets it. By saying that you know how important this need is and that you will do what you can to make sure she gets what she wants and needs, you are creating a compassionate, non-defensive conversation.

5. **Offer an alternative**. Instead of saying no outright, offer an alternative solution or plan. Then *breathe*. Do not say anything more. This is about saying no with compassion. You want your parent, spouse, or child to hear first what you will do, *not* what you won't or can't do. You are taking charge of the message you are delivering.

6. **Do *not* explain, defend, or justify.** This step is especially challenging for most people, not just caregivers. We've been taught to have a good reason for doing, or not doing, something. In school, teachers ask for your reasoning; parents ask you for explanations; you yourself may have asked your children, spouses, employees, and colleagues for their explanations or reasoning in any given situation or circumstance. The problem with explaining, defending, or justifying is that you open yourself to a challenge or argument. While you may still get resistance or an argument, this is part of your pop quiz. Are you committed to your desired outcome? Do you still want or need to respond differently than you have in the past? Are you going to make your needs and feelings a priority? This is not about selfishness; it's about self-preservation. Should you get resistance to your new answer to your father's request, for example, you can go back to Step 4. You can still validate your father's needs and feelings and truly express compassion for what he is asking.

7. **Say thank you.** Even though your mother may feel upset, disappointed, or frustrated, say, "I understand this is different and I thank you for understanding. I appreciate it very much. It means a lot to me that I can handle your request this way." While your mother may not really be understanding or respectful of your new decision and response, when you express your gratitude, you are changing the dynamics of this conversation. Instead of communicating defensiveness and creating an argument, you are focusing on the desired outcome to take loving and respectful care of yourself.

When you are loving and respectful of yourself, you will be communicating in a way that sounds and seems loving and respectful to others as well. While this is a challenge and may feel daunting, think about how you have faced other challenges. Did they help you grow, and did you feel empowered by the results? Focus on your desired outcome and think about this challenge the way Steve Maraboli describes it in his book, *Unapologetically You: Reflections on Life and the Human Experience:* "Challenges in life can either enrich you or poison you. You are the one who decides."

The reality is, you do not have control over what the other person's reaction will be as you embark on this new part of your journey to self-care. All you control is how you choose to respond, and, if you handle yourself differently and with greater self-respect and care, then it is a job well done. This is yet another part of the pop quiz.

8. **Practice compassionate detachment.** Compassionate detachment means you let go from the outcome (or the other person's reaction). You can go through all the above steps and feel really good about what and how you communicated and still hit roadblocks. Your mission is to communicate your desired outcome, which you did. You do not have control over how someone else reacts or responds. This is challenging because, of course, we want everyone to be accepting of our newfound assertiveness. That, however, is not the goal. The goal is self-care, and we cannot control whether anyone will appreciate our changes.

This last step is about detaching from the outcome. If, or when, you come up against resistance to your change, repeat Step 4: Validate their feelings. Then review Step 5 by restating your alternative plan or solution. And once again, say thank you.

If an argument seems imminent, repeat Step 4 and, if you are on the phone, end the conversation with an "I love you, and I'll talk with you later." If you are face to face, state "I love you," and take a break by leaving the room. (Go to the bathroom; say you have to make a phone call; take a break). If your loved one seems particularly contentious, you can say, "I see how upset you are, and we can revisit this another time, but right now, I'm learning to do things that are for my greater good, so that I can lovingly do what I need to do to help and care for you."

The steps take courage. Pop quizzes bring you the opportunity to make changes that allow you to take as good care of yourself as you do of others in your life. If your habit has been to worry about how everyone else feels and their needs, then you have been undermining and sabotaging yourself. Why has it been acceptable to put your needs and feelings on hold while you lovingly and devotedly care for everyone else? At what cost to your health, well-being, relationships, and quality of life? Remember the importance of putting the oxygen mask over *your* face first.

Making changes and dealing with pop quizzes does *not* mean you are saying "no" all the time, nor does it mean you are now saying that someone else's needs and feelings no longer matter. This is about understanding that your needs and feelings matter just as much as anyone else's. It is necessary that you do things that take care of you in order to prevent compassion fatigue and burnout and the physical and emotional problems that result from providing the ongoing care for others that has seemingly taken over your life.

Pop quizzes allow you the opportunity to check in and assess whether or not, in any given moment, you are paying attention to your needs. Every moment is a learning opportunity. You can do the same thing and keep hoping for a different result, and we know where that leads, or you can use each pop quiz as an opportunity to make changes.

It is important that you not judge yourself when these pop quizzes show up in your life. You are learning new thoughts, new beliefs, and new behaviors, and that takes practice, patience, perseverance, and courage in order to feel safe putting them into action with the people in your life. As Mary Anne Radmacher wrote, "Courage doesn't always roar. Sometimes courage is the little voice at the end of the day that says I'll try again tomorrow."

I KNOW AND UNDERSTAND HOW hard it is to make changes and deal with the never-ending and often daunting emotional pop quizzes that show up in life. You have thought it was all on you and that you had no choice but to keep on keeping on; this book is your reminder that you have options, and you can have support, guidance, and encouragement to access the courage that lives inside. You can start today, because whether you do things differently today or not, those pop quizzes will keep on coming; that's life.

And we breathe…

Chapter 9 Worksheet

Pop Quizzes: Oops, It Happened Again

In life, good experiences will produce memorable moments, bad experiences will produce lessons.

—*Anonymous*

THIS WORKSHEET WILL HELP YOU handle the moments that challenge you, upset you, and catch you by surprise.

1. What feelings are being brought up by this situation, for me?

   _____

   _____

   _____

2. What thoughts or beliefs are being brought up by this situation, for me?

   _____

   _____

   _____

3. Can I use this pop quiz to practice being more loving and respectful of myself? What action can I take or what message can I deliver?

   _____

   _____

   _____

4. Am I ready to focus on a desired outcome that encourages my growth and change?

_____

   a. My *reaction* to the event:

   _____

   _____

   _____

   b. My *response* to the event:

   _____

   _____

   _____

Notice the difference between reacting versus responding. Which leads you closer to achieving your desired outcome?

5. Is my desire for a new outcome stronger than my fear of someone else's reaction?

_____

6. If I need additional support to deal with this pop quiz, to whom can I reach out?

_____

To create more positive results in your life, replace
"if only" with "next time."

—*Anonymous*

More Tools for Change:
Affirmations for Pop Quizzes

MANY POP QUIZZES ARE LESSONS learned after the fact. In school we get the lesson and then the quiz; in life, we get the quiz and then we get the lesson. Here is an affirmation you may find useful when you get your next pop quiz:

It's not the issue that arises that matters;
it's how I deal with it, what I learn from it,
and how I apply that lesson to my life.

If we are not allowed to deal with small problems, we will be destroyed by slightly larger ones. When we come to understand this, we live our lives not avoiding problems, but welcoming them as challenges that will strengthen us so that we can be victorious in the future.

—Jim Stovall, *The Ultimate Gift*

Chapter 10
Siblings Without Rivalry

*I want a relationship where we talk like best
friends, play like kids, argue like husband and wife,
and protect each other like siblings.*

—*Anonymous*

THERE ARE DOZENS OF BOOKS about sibling relationships, and this chapter is simply a place to start as you create healthier communication in the process of caring for your parent(s). From the perspective and purpose of this book, to help you take as good care of yourself as you do of others in your life, I offer you a framework from which you can move forward in a healthy, empowered, and meaningful way when dealing with your parents' needs and your relationship with your brothers and sisters.

Sibling relationships have long histories and therefore long-standing expectations, patterns of behavior, and beliefs about who each of you are. For many people, communicating with sisters and brothers in the process of addressing all the responsibilities of caregiving for parents can seem like navigating through a minefield.

Some of the issues that need to be considered before we take on any conversation when it comes to the care that your parent(s) receive are:

- Who lives closest to Mom and Dad?
- If everyone lives nearby, is there clear communication as to who does what?
- If everyone lives far away, is there agreement about care, visits, and hiring help?
- Who is used to being in charge?
- Who has primary responsibility for their care?
- What were your relationships like as you were growing up?
- Do you really know and understand who you all are today?
- Were there rifts in relationships with each other or with Mom and Dad or both that pre-date their current care needs?
- Are the financial circumstances for your parents and any siblings or both an issue?
- What are each sibling's personal needs and other life commitments that must be taken into consideration?

Obviously there are many questions and many potential points of challenge or support, and most will be based on what your history has been. Navigating through relationships and life is easy when life is easy, it's said. Though caregiving may start out as easy, after any length of time it doesn't necessarily stay that way.

When it comes to dealing with major challenges such as chronic uncooperativeness, a shutdown in communication, too much animosity, or strongly differing opinions that cannot be resolved, there's always the option of elder mediation. Mediation with a professional, objective third party is less costly than formal litigation with an attorney, where all parties involved must hire attorneys. Also, because the mediation approach and process are quite different from litigation, you may ultimately feel more respect for each other, achieve more civility on an ongoing basis, and ultimately create the best possible outcome for your parent(s) and yourselves.

In a number of families I have worked with, where siblings are living around the country, engaged on different levels with their parents, and still wanting to have a say in how Mom or Dad is cared for, tensions rise and anger flares. The primary caregiver has ended up feeling defensive, angry, and resentful during their conversations with their siblings. On many occasions I've heard clients tell me that they just want their siblings to spend *even one day* handling what they deal with every day instead of barking orders, complaining, judging, and criticizing.

They struggle to stay calm during conversations and not get overly defensive about their management of Mom's affairs when siblings come to visit and point out things they believe should be done differently, such as how Mom's medications are organized, how the house is organized, what activities Mom should participate in to help her to be more active and engaged. The list can be long and nitpicky. Arguments have ensued regarding clearing out the clutter of the house or who gets to inherit which items Mom or Dad no longer need or want. In other words, the pressures mount and relationships feel increasingly frayed.

> Our siblings push buttons that cast us in roles we felt sure we had let go of long ago—the baby, the peacekeeper, the caretaker, the avoider… It doesn't seem to matter how much time has elapsed or how far we've traveled.
>
> —Jane Mersky Leder, *The Sibling Connection*

Regardless of the myriad issues that come up in your role as caregiver, it's important to remember to deal with only one issue or topic at a time; otherwise you will feel chaotic and become distracted and overwhelmed.

Start by laying out the following rules for family meetings:

1. **Focus on only one issue at a time.** Get clarity on the issue to be discussed. Otherwise, given the myriad issues that come up in your role as caregiver, things will feel chaotic as people become distracted by their pet peeves and hot-button issues.

2. **And we breathe.** Ensure that you feel calm and centered. Know that there is no rush and slow down if anyone starts to seem overwhelmed.

3. **Define the desired outcome.** The overarching desired outcome may be to take the best possible care of Mom, and there may be a variety of ideas and possibilities to achieve this goal. Each person gets to state what he or she believes is the best plan.

4. **Only one person speaks at a time.** You have to take turns. Remind each other: "Your needs and feelings are as important to you as my needs and feelings are to me."

5. **Take notes.** This helps prevent reacting, maintains clarity on what is being said and what the issues and concerns are for each person, and shows respect for what is being said.

6. **No judgments.** Simply list everyone's ideas without criticism or judgments. View it as a "brainstorming" session, in which all ideas are included for consideration in the discussion to follow.

7. **Review ideas and possibilities that have been shared.**
   Make sure that you (or whoever has been designated note-taker) captured all the ideas that were shared.
8. **Engage in calm and respectful dialogue.** Continue until agreements are made about who will do what and how.

The following scenario is similar to stories a number of people have shared with me regarding communicating with siblings about caring for their mother.

Isabel is one of four children and lives in a two-family house with their mother, who is physically frail but mentally alert. She is also frequently cranky, resentful of the care she needs, and resistant to participating in social activities with other seniors. Mom spends most of her days home alone except for visits from aides a few hours a day, visits from Isabel (who often works from home), and occasional phone calls from her other three children.

Most evenings, because Mom is by herself, Isabel has dinner and watches TV with her, then helps her get ready for bed. Isabel rarely goes out with friends because she doesn't want to leave Mom home alone. A widow, Isabel has a daughter, son-in-law, and granddaughter who live about three hours away.

In the situation in question, Isabel wanted to take a week off to visit her daughter and granddaughter, whom she hadn't seen in about six months. She was feeling angry and resentful that none of her siblings had ever offered to relieve her, to give her some time off.

We worked on preparing for the conference call Isabel planned to have with her siblings so that she could ask for what she wanted and needed. Yes, Isabel would have loved to have had them *offer* to relieve her, but since that hadn't ever happened, it was time for her to change the pattern and her expectations, and *ask* them.

Isabel sent an email setting up the time for the conference call and laid out the rules so that they could all be on the same page. She told them in the email that there was an issue she wanted their input on with regard to Mom and that she hoped they could work together to resolve it. In the email she thanked them for all their anticipated help knowing how much they all loved Mom and wanted what was best for her. She asked one of her sisters if she'd be willing to take notes, so they could all look forward to having the information discussed and not worry about remembering everything.

The day and time were set.

Isabel practiced being able to say clearly and directly what she wanted and needed, without defensiveness, resentment, or fear leaking into her words.

Here are the steps that worked really well for her, resulting in a respectful and very productive flow of helpful dialogue:

1. **Say thank you.** Starting with gratitude is important for you as well as your siblings as it sets the tone for the conversation.

2. **State the issue clearly, directly and without apology.** "I want to plan to visit my daughter and granddaughter and Mom needs coverage while I'm away."

3. **State what you need or want**. Clearly and directly, ask your siblings for what you want. Remember that if you don't ask, the answer is always no. Often siblings don't offer to help because they are used to you handling everything

and no longer think about your needs or what else they could do to help.

4. **Take nothing personally.** Even when her siblings didn't jump in to help or offer ideas, Isabel was able to breathe calmly. She reminded herself that they weren't being inconsiderate of her, that they had to figure out their lives and how to accommodate the change she was asking for. She then asked what ideas they had so that she could get away for the week. They ultimately came up with a couple of ideas, including: "Take Mom with you," or, "Have your daughter come to you." Isabel offered the ideas of respite care at a local facility, having aides stay with mom all day every day, having any one of her siblings come and stay for the week, or dividing the week up among them.

5. **Maintain compassionate detachment.** Without any judgments, Isabel steeled herself to stay calm and wait to see what ideas her siblings would agree to. She stayed focused on her desired outcome and was not concerned about which option her siblings chose. This was a major milestone for Isabel, as she allowed herself to relinquish control to push for any one solution. She knew she needed to leave this issue to her siblings. (The only ideas Isabel did not want to consider were taking mom with her or having her daughter come to her. Isabel wanted *time off*.)

6. **Implement the plan.** Once her siblings determined that they could, in fact, visit their mother, they all chose the week Isabel could be away and they worked out the days each of them would come to stay with Mom.

7. **Celebrate.** Once a desired outcome is achieved, even if it isn't ideal, celebrate that a change has been made and that this is a success you can build on in the future. Isabel thanked everyone for being willing to participate and asked her sister who was taking notes to please send a follow-up email confirming the dates so that they'd all be clear on what they had agreed to.

Of course not all conversations go smoothly, and there can be bumps in the road. It may even take more than one conversation to achieve a desired outcome. It's important to remember that communicating in a new way with your siblings to establish new rules and boundaries takes courage, practice, patience, and a lot of perseverance. With a plan, clarity, and a willingness to stay focused on your self-care and the fact that you do indeed matter, successes on many levels can and will be achieved.

And we breathe…

Chapter 10 Worksheet

Siblings Without Rivalry

1. Describe each of my siblings and their qualities, those I like and admire and those I dislike, feel intimidated by, resent, and the like.

   _____

   _____

   _____

2. How am I seen in my relationship with my siblings (one to be ignored, challenged, the boss, the baby, distant, the problem, and so on)? Is this how I want to be seen?

   _____

   _____

   _____

   _____

   _____

3. How do I see my siblings' roles and relationships with me and with our parents?

   _____

   _____

   _____

   _____

4. What is my desired outcome in terms of my relationship with my siblings?

_____

_____

_____

_____

5. What are the primary issues we have to address in order to best care for Mom and/or Dad?

_____

_____

_____

_____

6. Am I willing to let go of past beliefs and judgments in order to best care for myself and my parents with the love, respect, and compassion we all deserve? (Review chapters on boundaries, anger, and forgiveness.)

_____

_____

_____

_____

7. Do we need professional mediation, and am I willing to suggest this option?

_____

_____

_____

Chapter 11
And We Breathe:
Breathing to Enhance Life

Breathing may be considered the most important
of all the functions of the body, for, indeed, all the
other functions depend upon it.

—*Yogi Ramacharaka,* Science of Breath

IT IS NOT ENOUGH TO breathe simply to sustain your life, we can also breathe to attain focus, clarity, and serenity. Practicing the breathing I've alluded to throughout this book and work on more fully here really can do all that and more!

Oxygen is the most vital nutrient for our bodies; without it we all know that death will occur within just a few minutes. That said, too many people have forgotten how to breathe to enhance their lives, so most people breathe simply to sustain life. When you are stressed, worried, focused, scared, tense, anxious, and so on, you tend to tighten up all over. Your shoulders rise up, your neck shrinks down, your jaws clench, and your abdominal muscles contract. You might also experience tightening of your arms and legs. In other words, every part of your body contracts and becomes constricted. (This is referred to as the "turtle mode"). When this happens, your breathing becomes shallow, and you start to feel fatigued due to oxygen deprivation in the blood because you have, literally, almost stopped breathing.

I hear all the time from clients, family, and friends that, as their stress, tension, responsibilities, anxieties, and worries increase, they have no time to breathe. As they continue to breathe in this constricted manner, it becomes increasingly evident that they're more irritable, stressed, and feel less able to concentrate, or they suffer from what is referred to as "general malaise."

While you may continue to blame your circumstances for this condition, it has been shown that, when you don't breathe effectively, you are not taking in sufficient oxygen and you are not eliminating sufficient carbon dioxide. As a result, your body becomes oxygen starved, and a toxic buildup of carbon dioxide occurs. Every cell in your body requires oxygen, and your level of vitality is a result of the total level of the health of all the cells. Additionally, shallow and rapid breathing do not exercise the lungs enough, so they lose some of their function, causing a further reduction in your overall feeling of health and vitality. Caregiving is stressful in and of itself, and it adds to your already busy and often overwhelming life. You have a lot going on in your life, and some of your stress is exacerbated in part because you are not really breathing deeply enough.

Remember that breathing is available all day, every day; oxygen is around you in abundance, and it's free. It really can be simple to do something that will help you to de-stress and reap the rewards of adding a free, healthy, and guilt-free new habit to your life.

Take a moment now as you're reading and stretch your arms up and over your head and as you extend your arms outward, lift your head up. As you do this take a deep breath and say out loud: "I am coping with my life with open arms." Follow this with another slow, deep breath. Allow yourself to feel what happens internally as you do this. As you become less contracted and constricted physically, your mind also opens to new possibilities for handling your concerns, stresses, and worries.

When you *Stop! Breathe! Focus!* you feel less stressed and less anxious in the moment, and when you breathe slowly and deeply and really fill your lungs, you are giving yourself the gift of additional health benefits. Breathing effectively steps up your metabolism, uses muscles that improve your posture, and keeps your lung tissue elastic, so you can then take in more oxygen. A good, slow, deep breath helps to tone your abdominal muscles and strengthens your immune system. I realize that it may be hard to believe that changing how you breathe could do so much for you, but it can and it does. When you concentrate on your breathing and breathe slowly and deeply, you can even improve your sleep.

Did you ever really consider how important breathing is? Most people don't, since it's something they do all the time without having to think about it. Paying attention to your breathing is an important part of living consciously and purposefully. It takes twenty-eight days to make a habit, so you can start today with practicing the new habit of life-enhancing breathing.

Three Steps to Life-Enhancing Breathing:

1. **Square breathing.** Once every hour, *Stop! Breathe! Focus!* Breathe in slowly and deeply through your nose to the count of four, hold your breath to the count of four and

release it gently with a sigh through your mouth to the count of four, then pause to the count of four. Repeat this pattern for sixty seconds, then return to your activity with renewed energy and clarity. (This is also called box breathing; in the military it's called tactical breathing.)

2. ***Stop! Breathe! Focus!*** Whenever you feel stressed, worried, upset, and so on, focus your eyes straight ahead or tilt your head back, stretch your arms open wide, take a slow, deep breath, and say aloud, "I am coping with my life with open arms." Feel your chest expand, your back muscles stretch, and your entire upper body open up. Repeat this process and the phrase three times. Then allow yourself to refocus on the issue that had stressed you or worried you. Notice the shift that occurs in how you look at the situation.

3. **Practice deep breathing.** Do this when you can sit or lie down comfortably with your back straight. Place your hands on your abdomen. As you breathe in, keep your shoulders and chest relaxed and focus on getting your breath to push out against your hands as your diaphragm and abdomen expand. (I know that most people have been taught to keep their stomachs in and their chests out, but that style does not promote deep breathing.)

Acknowledge that you're going against old messages; that it's okay and that it's for your greater good. As you breathe in, feel your abdomen expand and, as you slowly release your breath, feel your abdomen release and relax as your breath moves slowly up and out of your mouth. You can apply gentle pressure on your abdomen to release the last of your breath. Repeat this process daily, but with just four to five deep breaths at any given sitting. This is a new experience, and, if your body isn't used to it, you may feel dizzy from all the oxygen flowing through you.

While breathing doesn't change the situations you're dealing with, it does give you an opportunity to change how you respond to them, and it absolutely does have an impact on your overall health and vitality.

This book is all about ways to take as good care of yourself as you do of others in your life. Breathing is an ever-important step in this process. Throughout every chapter there have been references to breathing and the fact that when you make the first step in any situation to *breathe*, you will give yourself the gift of being better able to respond rather than react.

Marjorie's Story

MARJORIE WAS RESPONSIBLE FOR EVERYONE in her life from the time she was a young girl. She took on enormous burdens when she should have been allowed to go out and play, be with friends, date, and just be a child. Marjorie learned to be responsible, and this was the essence of her belief, her behaviors, and her habits. It never occurred to her that she had any choice. Whether it was family, friends, work, or church, if there was a need, Marjorie filled it. She did this for years without thinking and without giving thought to whether or not jumping in and fixing, rescuing, and taking care was a good thing.

While the issues we discussed included setting boundaries, focusing on a desired outcome, and exploring options, the first thing Marjorie had to learn was to *breathe*. Before Marjorie could make any new choices, she had to practice slowing down her reaction time. Breathing before responding took time, patience, and a lot of practice. There were many opportunities for her to persevere in learning how to short-circuit her automatic yes to everyone and everything. Breathing was that step to change a lifelong habit.

For a long time, Marjorie practiced breathing without changing her answers to everyone's requests. This is normal. The shift in her responses began to occur as Marjorie became aware of her feelings about requests, because she took the time to breathe, notice her feelings, and realize that she might be allowed to make a different decision regarding the requests being made. This was a huge aha moment for her.

Practicing breathing helped Marjorie move forward on her journey to taking as good care of herself as she did (and had been doing) of everyone else in her life. Life-enhancing breathing helped Marjorie literally take a breath, and that took her out of autopilot mode and helped her move into a conscious, mindful mode.

Do not underestimate the importance of this one shift in your life. It is challenging to embrace and practice all the steps I've outlined in this book. My desired outcome is to provide information, guidance and support for you to live your life empowered and fulfilled while still providing loving care to those in your life. Breathing to enhance your life is at the core of every self-care strategy.

Do yourself the favor of taking care of yourself with the love, respect, and compassion you deserve and add life-enhancing breathing to your life. *And we breathe…* gives you pause so that you can face your day, your decisions, and your life from a more conscious, relaxed, purposeful, and healthy space. You deserve to take back your life.

And we breathe…

Chapter 11 Worksheet

And We Breathe: Breathing to Enhance Life

BREATHING PRACTICES THAT WILL AID in de-stressing and calming your feelings and thoughts:

Square breathing (box breathing or tactical breathing)

1. Inhale slowly and deeply through your nose for the count of four.
2. Hold your breath for the count of four.
3. Exhale gently with a sigh through your mouth for the count of four.
4. Pause for the count of four.
5. Repeat steps 1 through 4 four times.

Advanced relaxation response breathing

1. Inhale slowly and deeply, resting your tongue on the roof of your mouth, for the count of four.
2. Hold for the count of seven while keeping your tongue on the roof of your mouth.
3. Exhale gently with a sigh through your mouth for the count of eight, while relaxing your tongue.
4. Rest for the count of four.
5. Repeat all steps four times.

And we breathe

1. When faced with a stressful or challenging moment, take a slow, deep breath while saying the phrase: "And we breathe…"
2. Repeat as needed, giving yourself time and space to review and decide: What's my desired outcome?

Slow deep breath

1. Open your arms wide and lift your head.
2. Say, "I am coping with my life with open arms."
3. End with a slow deep breath.
4. Repeat these steps four times and feel the shift in your thoughts and energy.

When life is foggy, path is unclear and mind is dull,
remember your breath. It has the power to give
you the peace. It has the power to resolve the
unsolved equations of life.

—*Amit Ray,* Beautify your Breath,
Beautify your Life

And we breathe…

More Tools for Change: Affirmations to Practice in Challenging Moments
Who I Am Is Enough

And we breathe... I move from reacting to responding. This gives me pause.

I remember to put my oxygen mask on first, so that I am able to take as good care of myself as I do of others. This is *not* selfishness, it is self-preservation.

I focus on my desired outcome. It is what I *want*, not what I *don't* want, and it is something over which I have control.

I acknowledge that *I matter*, and that my needs and feelings count.

I set and maintain boundaries because this is my sign of self-respect.

I communicate my needs, feelings, and thoughts to others with love, respect, and compassion.

I say no with compassion. I offer alternatives when I can and I do not explain, defend, or justify.

I deserve to create and feel ease within my days and in my life. By taking care of myself with love, respect, and compassion, I am better able to provide the same to others.

I breathe through my fears and allow myself to make changes that are for my greater good.

Dealing effectively with my anger or resentment is an *A.R.T.* It requires Acceptance, Respect, and Time to process.

Forgiveness is a gift I give myself. I choose to look for loving intentions from others and within myself.

Asking for and receiving help from others is *not* a sign of weakness or failure. It helps me create greater balance in my life.

Pop quizzes are learning opportunities often disguised as gifts in black wrapping as I learn to take as good care of myself as I do of those I love.

I call and reach out for support, guidance, and learning so that I really can take as good care of myself as I do of others in my life.

And we breathe…

And Life Goes On…

WHILE I HAVE ALWAYS SEEN myself as a caregiver, from childhood through my career, my marriage, and as a parent and addressing the needs my parents had, my awareness and passion for self-care has most definitely evolved. I never thought about my needs being important until I saw and felt what happened when I was living on a back burner. I created the Take Back Your Life: Art of

Self-Care group because I learned how important it was to have guidance, support, and encouragement to step out of isolation and martyrdom. One does not grow and learn alone.

I am blessed to be part of caregivers' lives as they learn, grow, and evolve in being able to reach out to others, step out of isolation and overwhelm, and ask for and receive the help we all need and deserve. I learned a long time ago that we teach what it is we need to learn and, working with caregivers for years, I have found greater awareness and learning every day. Participants in our group share the blessings and benefits they have derived from having a space that is just for them.

Change in our lives is possible if we allow it. I dreamt about creating a group for caregivers because I know how important connections and connecting are. Group participants share with me, and each other, the benefits they reap and I am grateful that Take Back Your Life: Art of Self-Care is a strong emotional resource for them, and can be for you as well.

Learning is never a straight line, and we all need a space where we can share our challenges, pitfalls, pop quizzes, and successes in an environment that is safe, supportive, helpful, and confidential. Everyone needs a space like this because life is all about learning new and more effective ways of dealing with stress, and caregivers' stress is high. As the saying goes, "stress is a given, suffering is optional." This program is a resource that helps eliminate suffering.

And we breathe...

Appendix 1

Caregiver's Step-by-Step Home Study
Take Back Your Life Guide

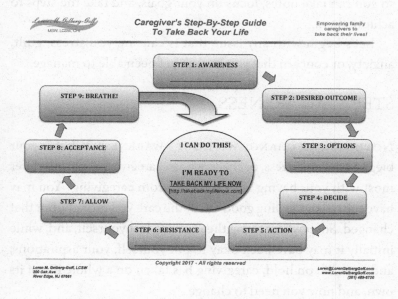

Loren M. Gelberg-Goff
MSW, LCSW, CPA

**Caregiver's Step-By-Step Guide
To Take Back Your Life**

Empowering family
caregivers to
take back their lives!

STEP 1: AWARENESS

STEP 9: BREATHE!

STEP 2: DESIRED OUTCOME

STEP 8: ACCEPTANCE

I CAN DO THIS!

**I'M READY TO
TAKE BACK MY LIFE NOW**
[http://takebackmylifenow.com]

STEP 3: OPTIONS

STEP 7: ALLOW

STEP 4: DECIDE

STEP 6: RESISTANCE

STEP 5: ACTION

Loren M. Gelberg-Goff, LCSW
200 Oak Ave
River Edge, NJ 07661

Loren@LorenGelbergGoff.com
www.LorenGelbergGoff.com
(201) 489-8720

THANK YOU FOR HAVING THE desire and courage to dive deeper into making changes in your life. You realize you need to do something different so you can live without guilt or resentment as you take back your life.

Since you are one of forty-three million family caregivers who strive every day to take care of someone you love, this Caregiver's Step-by-Step Guide is how to begin learning to take as good care of yourself as you do of those you love.

Instructions on airplanes say that, should oxygen be required, and you are traveling with someone you are caring for, you should place an oxygen mask over your own face first. In life, as on planes, if you are not ensuring your well-being, those you care for cannot thrive.

Fill in the blanks on the guide itself or use a sheet of paper so you can take notes, focus on your goals, and take the steps to achieve them.

Let's begin with any issue that is causing you stress, guilt, anxiety, or concern that you haven't yet been able to manage.

STEP 1: AWARENESS

NOTHING CAN CHANGE WITHOUT AWARENESS. What is your biggest concern, stress, or challenge as a caregiver? What interferes most with your having a life separate from caregiving? You may have started out feeling good about the care you provide, but that changed. Somewhere along the way, you lost yourself, and, while initially it may have been okay to put yourself, your aspirations, and your life on hold, caregiving has taken on a whole life of its own, and now you need to change.

Awareness is moving out of autopilot mode into conscious decision-making mode. You acknowledge you need something different, but you're not quite sure a) that you are able, b) that you're allowed, or c) that you would even know how to bring this change about.

Now there's an internal conflict. Part of you wants a change, and part of you is resigned to life as it is—the part of you that feels powerless to change because Mom (or Dad or spouse or child) needs so much, and there's just no other way. I know this feels totally overwhelming, but here's where our work begins.

That other part of you is calling to you, screaming to you, or even crying: *Please find a way.*

Maybe this awareness didn't originate from within you; maybe someone in your family spoke up, telling you it's not fair that you're not available anymore or that you've lost your sense of humor. Whatever the catalyst, you now have awareness, and that's the first step. So, what are you most aware of? What is your biggest challenge or concern? Write it (or them) down, and we'll define your desired outcome.

First, state a desired outcome in terms of *what you want*, not what you don't want. Whatever we direct our attention to grows bigger. Suppose I tell you, "Don't think about pink elephants; absolutely, under no circumstances, think about pink elephants." What goes through your mind? Pink elephants. Our psyches do not connect to the negative. Focus on what you want: I want a weekend off; I want to be able to schedule time at the gym; I want to have lunch with a friend; I want a date night with my spouse; I want more ease and peace in my life; and so on.

What do you *really* want? If your biggest concern is that you have no free time, or that you have no time to schedule your own doctor appointments, or that you are constantly canceling plans with friends because of your mother's needs and demands, then maybe what you really want is a day for you to take care of you.

Think about how important this desired outcome is. Has it been on a back burner for a long time? Is it something you thought was out of the realm of possibility? Yes, you can have more than one desired outcome. Make no judgments as to what you want. Get in touch with what you *do* want. You cannot get to a desired outcome without awareness of what you are feeling, missing, needing, and wanting.

Secondly, a desired outcome must be something you control. It cannot be "I want my mother to be understanding," since you don't control how Mother will behave. You only control your own behavior and attitude, so your desired outcome might be expressed as: "I want to express my thoughts, opinions, needs or feelings in a way that will be clear, direct and compassionate." As long as you focus on someone else's reactions or attitudes or behaviors, you give up on your own needs and feelings, further undermining your care and self-worth. Having a desired outcome and honoring it means you will be open to finding a way.

STEP 2: POSSIBILITIES

WHAT CHOICES DO YOU HAVE? List all the ways you've handled this issue. They remain options even if they are ones you no longer like or that no longer give you the results you want.

And now, write down new possibilities, new ideas, new options, even if they seem outrageous and not possible, even if they're ideas you've dismissed in the past because someone would be upset. Write them down anyway. Think outside the box. First, think about *you*! You cannot explore your possibilities and options if you remain attached to someone else's opinions, feelings, or fears. You've been stuck; now see your way to something new, different, and ultimately to a better quality life.

If others do not like a change in you, it's because they are used to you behaving in a way that is familiar and that works for them. Change always brings about some discomfort. You are aware of the discomfort in your life created by dealing with this situation as you always have. Which discomfort you are willing to deal with: the same old, same old, or something that will bring you closer to your desired outcome?

Are you fearful that your new possibilities may not give you the results you hope for? You don't know how something will work out, but you *do* know how things have been working. You are aware that something isn't uplifting, empowering, and hopeful. Let's create new possibilities.

STEP 3: DECIDE

PICK A POSSIBILITY. COMMIT TO the choice that will move you toward your desired outcome. Take a deep breath and let that decision settle into your system. Feel whatever discomfort you may feel and remind yourself: *It's not my feelings that get me into trouble, it's my actions.* Making a decision means you begin to think about yourself and your life in a new way—with new energy and new perspectives.

Your decision is not written in stone. Each new decision brings you new direction, and each new reaction you feel or receive from others means you get to go back to Step 1 and process how you want to handle this new awareness. Your choices and decisions can change as you move forward.

When we don't know what we want, it's much harder to make a decision. Every time you allow yourself to become aware, to stop and breathe, you allow yourself the opportunity to think about your desired outcome: Who are you taking care of, and are you, in fact, putting your oxygen mask on yourself first?

Looking at the decision of your choice, fill in one step you will take to honor your decision. Just one step can make all the difference between same old, same old and something new, something you want, need, and deserve to take back your life. Every decision you make requires some action. Action moves beyond the *wish* for what you want toward making it a reality.

For example, if you decide that you need help to do the grocery shopping for your mother, you list your options to make this happen. You decide to order groceries online, so, one step could be setting up an online account at the local grocery store. If you decide that you would prefer to ask a sibling to do the shopping, one step might be writing a script so you can practice asking before you make the actual call. Maybe you decide to ask a member of your church or synagogue for help. You could write a request for your minister or rabbi to announce to the congregation or an announcement for the congregation newsletter.

Take one step, and each step will lead to the next, so that you feel yourself moving to achieve your desired outcome. Once that first step is completed, breathe, check how you feel, and prepare yourself for the next step. You are becoming increasingly aware, in touch, and committed to your desired outcome. And yet you still feel shaky, a little uncertain. After all, this is new territory, and old beliefs and habits keep popping up.

STEP 4: RESISTANCE

WHAT THOUGHTS MAKE YOU WANT to ignore your awareness, new possibilities, and your decision? Taking action means you are moving out of your comfort zone. Maybe you are telling yourself:

It's not worth it; siblings will be upset; Mom doesn't like anyone else to help her; I'll feel like a failure if I ask for help. The chatter of negative messages and beliefs goes on and on. Success lies just outside your comfort zone.

Simply breathe and acknowledge that you are doing something new and different, and it is normal to feel uncertain. Maybe you also feel a sense of relief and a feeling of freedom, and that triggers feelings of guilt. You are challenging the status quo, and it is uncomfortable at the start. Breathe through your resistance.

STEP 5: ALLOW

ALLOW FEELINGS TO FLOW THROUGH you and recognize that all changes require a period of adjustment. Focus on the feelings that arise as you choose to shift your behavior and outlook. Take time to let that shift, that idea, thought, attitude, settle in. Are you willing to allow yourself time to adjust to your new choices? Fill in the blank line: Yes.

Some questions to think about are: Am I really willing to allow for changes in my behaviors, attitude and beliefs? Am I really willing to admit that my needs and feelings matter? Am I willing to allow new possibilities into my life? Am I willing to deal with others' reactions?

You will find increased awareness, not only of your own feelings, but of attitudes and behaviors you have been tolerating in others that have had a negative impact on your self-esteem, self-confidence, and self-care.

STEP 6: ACCEPTANCE

DO YOU DESERVE THIS GREATER good and your overall health and wellness? If you still feel doubt or uncertainty, go back to Steps 2 through 5. I know these changes can feel overwhelming; that's what a step-by-step guide is for, and why I offer ongoing support. Are you willing to observe and allow others' reactions to your new behavior without giving in to them? Fill in the blank line: Yes.

Accept doesn't mean *like*. You may know that you have to accept a new attitude, perspective, or behavior in your life, but you may still think it's not fair that you're the one doing all the work to improve your life and the lives of the people you care for.

Acceptance means you decide how best to take as good care of yourself as you do of the others in your life. It doesn't mean resigning yourself to the same old, same old; it means acknowledging what the situation is that you cannot change (a parent's failing health, siblings who are not involved or who live too far away to help out on a day-to-day basis, or maybe you're the one who lives far away and you feel guilty about not helping out more). Whatever your situation, it must be accepted so that you can realistically decide what changes you can effect so that you feel healthier, more empowered, and more open to achieving a positive desired outcome. Take a deep breath and know you are moving forward on a path toward your desired outcome of less stress and greater ease.

STEP 7: AND WE BREATHE

BREATHING IS THE SINGLE MOST important thing you can do to get through your stress, tension, anxiety, anger, and frustration. Breathing gives you space from reacting so that you can respond thoughtfully, mindfully, and with clarity. *And we breathe* gives you pause, gives you the moment to become aware of what you are feeling, what you are thinking, and what it is you need or want.

Breathing is a simple, automatic function, and yet, when people are stressed, angry, frustrated, and overwhelmed, they actually stop breathing. *And we breathe* can become your mantra, your go-to phrase when you feel that jolt of upset, stress, or tension. Saying the phrase out loud will get you to take a good, deep breath and help you reset your internal system. It will help you stop reacting so you can respond thoughtfully. Take your time, process, and use this Caregiver's Step-by-Step Guide to achieve your desired outcome in any given situation.

Are you ready to breathe through your fear and uncertainty and let the new you settle in? Fill in the blank line: Yes.

At the Heart of Everything

LET ME NOW DIRECT YOUR attention to the middle of the Caregiver's Step-By-Step Guide—the bullseye—the heart of everything affecting you as a caregiver.

For those of you who are knee-deep in feeling the imbalance, the feeling of being overwhelmed and the stress and know you need a deeper level of support: You are aware that you need more than a do-it-yourself program. Consider taking one more step that will be meaningful and worthwhile for *yourself*.

After all, we cannot effectively give to those we love if we are not effectively caring for ourselves.

Ask yourself: What would it be like to have ongoing support so that you could wake up each day without feeling guilt, anger, or resentment as a caregiver?

Has going through this book increased your awareness? When is it *your* time? Are you ready to take one more action step to start taking back your life?

If so, say "Yes!" and write that down.

Let me share something with you: Caregivers *are* finding a way, having a life, catching a break, and breaking that cycle of guilt and feeling overwhelmed. It's the Take Back Your Life group program.

It's a meaningful, and yet simple, way to take care of yourself while reducing the pressure, stress, tension that affects you in your everyday life.

The Take Back Your Life group program covers exactly what is overwhelming you so you can:

- Get out of self-sabotage—stop doing the same things over and over again that don't work.
- Finally end self-deprivation—stop making yourself last on the list.
- Recognize the strong hold of guilt and discover powerful ways to eliminate it from your life.
- Start overcoming the daily resentment so you can enjoy time with your loved one again.

- Find the right way to deal with anger so you can find forgiveness and compassion for others and, most importantly, for yourself.

Do something for you. This is your next step.

My parting wish is for you, the caregiver, to find ease, to find joy again, and to begin today to take back your life.

And we breathe...

Appendix 2

Resources and References for Caregivers

HERE IS A LIST OF resources that are needed or may be needed as you care for your aging parent. I am not including links to these resources as the Internet is forever changing and links can become outdated. With access to a computer, however, you can search any of the following services or phrases and get the most up-to-date information. Therefore, the following list is to be used as a resource, helping you understand what to ask and who to ask for the assistance you need to provide care for your parents, allowing you to take as good care of yourself as you do of others in your life.

Aging Life Care Professional (formerly, Geriatric Care Manager)

THE AGING LIFE CARE PROFESSIONAL is educated and experienced in any of several fields related to aging life care and care management, including but not limited to nursing, gerontology, social work, or psychology, with a specialized focus on issues related to aging and elder care. They are experienced in addressing the concerns of families as trusted professional advisors and service providers. They will be able to refer you to trusted elder care attorneys and/or mediators based upon your specific needs and issues.

Elder Care Attorney

ELDER CARE ATTORNEYS ARE ADVOCATES for the elderly and their loved ones. Most elder law attorneys handle a wide range of legal matters affecting older or disabled persons, including issues related to health care, long-term care planning, guardianship, retirement, Social Security, Medicare/Medicaid, and other important issues relating to estate planning along with making referrals to Aging Life Care Professionals as well as elder mediators if needed or requested.

Elder Mediation

ELDER MEDIATION PROVIDES A FORUM for family decision-making. It is private, confidential, and completely voluntary. Elder mediators create an environment that supports and enhances conflict resolution and develops and improves communication strategies so that family members can successfully work together to make the important and necessary decisions regarding parents' care and needs. Mediators can facilitate referrals to Aging Life Care Professionals, elder care attorneys, assisted living facilities, and so on.

Transportation Resources

WHEN YOUR PARENTS CAN NO longer drive, there are options for arranging transportation for medical appointments, social engagements, shopping, and so on. Some may be covered by insurance. Search online for senior transportation or contact your local senior services agency.

Respite Care

THE EASYLIVINGFL.COM DEFINITION OF RESPITE care is "a short period of rest or relief from something difficult or unpleasant" or "an interval of rest or relief." Respite care generally offers this kind of a break to a primary caregiver. Respite might be provided full-time for a period such as a week or two (for example while a caregiver travels), or on an intermittent basis (such as every afternoon or once a week so the caregiver can run errands, rest, or attend an activity). Respite care is one option for caregivers to take care of themselves, and stay healthy and better able to continue caregiving.

Home Health Care

HOME HEALTH CARE INCLUDES A wide range of health care services that can be given in your home for an illness or injury. Home health care is usually less expensive, more convenient, and can be just as effective as care you get in a hospital or skilled nursing facility, depending on the physical, medical, mental, and emotional needs of your parent. Home care is the option chosen when there is a need or desire to have your parent cared for at home.

The Internet offers resources and articles on assessing home care agencies and assisted living facilities. (Check Public Broadcasting System, PBS, American Association of Retired Persons, AARP)

Assisted Living

AN ASSISTED LIVING RESIDENCE IS a long-term senior care option that provides personal care, support services such as meals, medication management, bathing, dressing, and transportation. Each state and province has different licensing and regulation requirements for assisted living providers, which affects the particular services offered within that community. In general, assisted living communities provide basic medical monitoring as well as daily activities and care. Activities of daily living include dressing, eating, mobility, hygiene, bathing, toileting, using the telephone, and shopping. It is often helpful to engage the services of an Aging Life Care Professional to help navigate the assisted living facilities in your area to find those that will best fit your parents' needs.

Adult Day Care Programs

ADULT DAY CARE CENTERS ARE designed to provide care and companionship for older adults who need assistance or supervision during the day. Programs offer relief to family members and caregivers, allowing them to go to work, handle personal business, or just relax while knowing their relative is well cared for and safe. The Department of Human Services offers lists of local day care programs, and Aging Life Care Professionals are a great resource for appropriate day programs that will meet your parents' needs.

Take Back Your Life: Art of Self-Care

THIS IS A TELEPHONE SUPPORT group that teaches, guides, and encourages caregivers to take as good care of themselves as they do of others in their lives. It reduces feelings of isolation and stress on the journey of caregiving. There is also a self-study program that is available to learn, practice changes and move forward at your own pace.

Acknowledgments

To my loving and supportive family, who constantly hold me accountable for all I do and encourage me every day to walk my talk: I am forever grateful for all you bring to my life.

This book would never have seen the light of day without the dedicated support and encouragement of Debra Angilletta of Angilletta Associates, my business mentor, guide, and steady hand for keeping me focused and inspired to complete this labor of love. You have been an amazing and brilliant gift in my life, and I am forever grateful.

To Lynn Crozier, whose writing and editing talents helped move this book forward: I am grateful and indebted to you for your support, input, and insights. Thank you for all you do to keep me on track. You are a vital asset to my life.

Thank you to my wonderful friend, Louise Mandelman, who was the first to go through this book with a fine-tooth comb. Thank you for your willingness to always be there for me and for your unwavering support. You are a dedicated and loving daughter and your caregiving journey has been a significant inspiration to me. I treasure our friendship and lifelong connection.

Thank you to my aunt, confidante, and lifelong supporter, Lillian Horwitz, LCSW. You mean more to me than you can imagine. Thank you for providing added insights for this book.

Thank you to my WIPO (Women who Inspire, are Profitable, and are Original) mastermind group. I am grateful for your support and encouragement along the way.

I thank Deborah Liss Fins, LICSW, CMC, and Aging Life Care Professional, whose insights and recommendations for this book made a difference; know that your friendship is a blessing in my life.

This book was brought to fruition with the added genius of AJ Harper, an amazing content and publishing strategist. I have learned so much from our work together that has made creating this book a remarkable journey.

Thank you to Bernadette Banci-Policastro. Your support, not only through this labor of love but through our life's challenges, and your understanding and priceless friendship, mean more to me than you will ever know.

Thank you to Amy Fuchs, LCSW, The Elder Expert, who was the first to encourage me to write this book, and has continued to be a supportive voice throughout the process of bringing this book to fruition.

Thank you, Lisa Albanese, who was with me on my weekend journey to write, write, write and gave me beautiful breaks as we toured Charleston, South Carolina. Your friendship and support for me (and Elliott) are priceless.

I give added thanks and much gratitude to the following people who were willing to read this book in its early stages and provide valuable input, ideas, recommendations, and testimonials: Dayna Desiderio-Orlak, Jeannie Senior, Gail Allen, Grace Ann Sweeney, Loretta Bleier, Donna Oriani, Peggy Larson, and Patricia Preztunik, owner of Bright Star Home Care in Emerson, New Jersey. I am truly grateful.

Thank you to Choi Messer, who wowed me with the cover of this book.

Thank you, Nicki Harper and Zoë Bird, for your valuable edits and input.

The Gelberg-Goff Family